TURNING
POINTS

Though this book is designed for group study, it is also intended for your personal enjoyment and spiritual growth. A leader's guide is available from your local bookstore or from your publisher.

TURNING POINTS

Beacon Hill Press of Kansas City
Kansas City, Missouri

Editor
Stephen M. Miller

Editorial Assistant
Rebecca Privett

Editorial Committee
Thomas Mayse
Stephen M. Miller
Carl Pierce
Gene Van Note
Lyle Williams

Copyright 1992

Printed in the United States of America
ISBN: 083-411-4011

Cover design by Ted Ferguson

CONTENTS

1

Honor the Father Who Abandoned Me?

"Look out the window,"
my aunt said.
"Your daddy is coming to see you."

by VaDonna Jean Leaf

MY FATHER abandoned my mother eight days before my birth, leaving us to years of struggle, want, and unhappiness.

I didn't hold anything against him through the painful years--no bitterness, no hatred or anger. In fact, there was a longing that grew into a compelling need to know him, to know about my grandparents, my great-grandparents—my genesis.

Attempts to find my father and his people were fruitless —until God unraveled the tangled webs.

I can still hardly believe how it all came about. Our children were grown when my husband, Paul, and I drove out of state on another search. We planned to scour records in the county seat near the town from which my grandmother had sent letters more than 50 years ago. All I had was a few names, a few places scattered in my memory, and the letters.

I knew my grandmother wouldn't be alive, but I hoped to find her grave and some information about a relative or family friend. Perhaps I could find a trace of my father, if he was living, or his grave if not.

The courthouse clerk stared at me, strangely, I thought. I was searching for my father, I said. When I mentioned names and relationships, she grew excited.

"I knew your grandmother, Sarrie!" she exclaimed. She talked of a cousin. "You look so much like her I thought you were her! That's why I stared so."

She knew my father as well. "He comes to see his sister pretty often," she said. "Did you know your aunt lives here in town?"

Things were happening too quickly. I remember walking down the steps, and I remember Paul driving to my aunt's house. I remember talking with her, but my mind was out of focus.

"Your daddy is staying with me," my aunt said. "He's been very sick and just out of the hospital. I'll talk to him. Go back to your motel and wait."

We did, and in what seemed like moments later the phone rang. "Look out the window," my aunt said. "Your daddy is coming to see you."

I was stunned. I watched a car drive up, watched a man get out. There was something familiar about him, something in his features.

Then suddenly, my father and I were face-to-face. How much alike our faces were.

The visit was stiff. We shook hands. I showed him a picture of his grandchildren. He shared bits of his life. He asked us to lunch, but I declined. I wouldn't be able to eat because of the excitement.

I asked why he had left. "They were hard years, the Depression," he said. He had had only a day job now and then, and no money. "Your mother said there had to be an operation. A thousand dollars.

"I didn't know what to do. I didn't intend to go away. I'd been looking for work every day. That particular day I was too ashamed to come back."

"Maybe we can write?" I ventured.

"Yes," he said. He gave me his address, but he didn't need mine! He knew where I lived. He'd known when I married, had known about our four children.

If he's kept tabs on me, I thought bitterly, why didn't he care enough to be a part of my life all those years? I ignored the anger. I was caught up in the day's amazement.

After the brief visit, my husband and I drove home. "All this is rather a shock," I wrote numbly in my diary.

In the days following I kept asking if the visit really happened, if I really had seen my father.

"It really happened," my husband said.

My mother burst into joyous tears when I told her. "I'm so glad you got to see your daddy," she said. I was her only child. She had gotten a divorce, married again, and made a new life.

When Daddy Cried

One day the telephone rang. "Hello. Do you know who this is?" While I puzzled at something familiar in the voice, he said, "This is your daddy," and he began to cry.

Letters came. "My life has changed since I met you," he wrote. "I think about you all the time. . . . I think about the past and how bad I was. . . . Will you forgive me?"

"I want to come and see you," he said on the phone one day. "I want to see my grandchildren."

His granddaughters, young adults now, welcomed him with kisses that brought a flood of tears. "I sure like my grandpa," his grandson said, summing up their feelings.

I liked him too. The bond between us grew.

There were more letters and daily telephone calls, sometimes three calls a day. There were many tears. He was sick and frightened; he felt lonely and abandoned. I knew the feeling well.

"My father called again today," I told Paul. "He wants to live with us."

"You helped take care of *my* mother and father, so it's only fair to help your parents." Paul's quick response told me he had already thought it out.

But I hadn't.

Our children were in college or careers. As our house emptied, I looked forward to interests I'd kept waiting on the back burner.

Caring for an elderly parent with health problems would mean new responsibilities and change. I told Dad he'd be moving from the busyness of the city, away from his friends. Would he be content with our quiet country home? Would he fit into our church life?

"It'll all work out," Paul said.

How could I doubt that, knowing God's hand had brought us together?

But I was skidding over a problem that was tightening in my chest.

In the beginning there had been no anger. To have found my father and feel the love blossoming between us was a dream come true. A constant prayer of praise sang in my heart, "Oh, thank You, God! Thank You."

But in the two visits, the many letters and phone calls, I picked up little things that slowly became hurts, jealousies, and resentments. A bitter root began to grow in me.

When he told me of his hard years, of being hungry, cold, of sleeping on the ground, I ached for him.

"Then," he said, "better times came." He talked about "my first new car," a second, a third; a trip taken, more trips, a camper, jewelry, gadgets. He'd worked hard and earned what he had . . . but I'd had so little.

All this had been going on in his life when I had appendicitis and mother had to "go to the county," as welfare was called, for help.

Mother had worried about my $12.00 graduation ring when my father bought himself a diamond ring.

He told about the year his mother died. I could have known my grandmother, I thought. I could have had my own memories of her.

I cried when he told me he once worked 15 miles from me. But the tears didn't help. I was angry. The bitter root continued growing.

If my father were to live with us, I had to forgive him.

I knew all about forgiving. I'd done it often. But I had been a wounded child, growing up when it was a disgrace not to have a complete family. I was shunned by community, school, and church, and had withered.

The hard feelings I might have felt toward my father I directed at others. They were there, they hurt me, they were part of my world; my father was not.

But now he was part of my life.

In the Lord's Prayer we ask to be forgiven as we forgive

others. Scripture tells us to forgive again and again; to put away bitterness, wrath, and anger; to be kind, tenderhearted, and forgiving.

These guidelines had worked for me before, even when I didn't feel like forgiving. I had learned to put forgiveness into words and prayer, then let feelings of forgiveness grow— slowly sometimes, and with struggle.

I had learned that without forgiveness, a hardness grows around the heart like a callus, holding back joy, peace, and healing, causing life to shrink. Now I had to draw on the source again.

I had found my father, and I couldn't bear to lose him again, this time to bitterness. I had to talk with him.

"You worked there, in that town, in other places close by, and you didn't come to see me?"

"No."

"That hurts."

"I tried to believe you weren't mine. I lived a lie. I knew when I made you. I know the day, the place.

"Every child needs a mother and a father. I know that now, but I didn't then."

A Bitter Root Dies

He told me of his father's death. "I hardly remember him," he said. "My mom was sick a lot. I felt myself a nuisance, in the way. I was sent to a sister here, a sister there, a brother, until I got old enough to take care of myself. Things happened. I was done wrong to. I couldn't trust people."

I learned his pattern of running away from hard things. It was the only way he knew to cope. He, too, had been hurt and wounded. As I pictured his life, I began to understand and to care.

"I wasn't a father to you," he said. "I failed you. I wish I could go back and correct the mistakes, but I can't." As we talked and cried together, the bitter root began to die.

But what about my mother?

I went to see her again. "My father wants to live with me and Paul."

A tear rolled down her cheek. "I've had you for 52 years. I think it would be wonderful that now your daddy can too."

Tears rushed to my eyes. Mother put aside all her years of sorrow. Could I be any less forgiving?

A few days later my father was hugged into our home.

It was a joyous time of forgiveness and love, a time to make up for the barren years. My father bloomed as father, father-in-law, and grandfather. He wept when he held his first great-grandchild. "What a pretty little face she has."

The first time my father went with us to my mother's house, there was a brief touching of hands, a tearing of the eyes. "I'm so sorry for all I've done," he said. Mother nodded, and that part of their lives was never spoken of again. My mother and stepfather came to our house; we went to theirs.

There came a day of a family reunion. "Many of Mother's people will be there," I told my father. "Would you like someone to come and stay with you while Paul and I go?"

"I'm going with you," he said. And he did, facing people he hadn't seen for years. As the branches of the family sorted themselves out, my father stood, said his name, and added, "VaDonna is my daughter."

I thought my heart would burst. In that moment I felt forgiving grace.

Sometimes I feel a great loss for those years of not knowing my father, my grandmother and cousins, and it overwhelms me. And I sometimes think about the escalating world of broken homes and unknown fathers; how a child, even a grown child, yearns for a father.

And fathers, too, yearn for their children. "There was always something I wanted, but I didn't know what it was until I saw you," he said. "Now at last I'm happy."

But God gave us even more happiness. I had the joy of holding my father's hands while he poured out his heart to God. "Oh, how I wish my dear little mama could know about this," he said afterward. "She prayed so much for me."

"She knows, Dad," I said.

Long ago in Sunday School a command was engraved upon my heart—not simply a lesson or a verse to memorize, but a command: " 'Honor your father and mother'—which is the first commandment with a promise" of blessing (Ephesians 6:2).

My father lived with us for five years before he died suddenly of heart failure in August 1985.

Six days before, he wrote a letter to a friend. "My daughter and her husband are so good to me. I'm happier now than I have ever been in my whole life."

I took my father in.

God blessed.

BACKGROUND SCRIPTURE: *Deuteronomy 5:16; Matthew 6:12-15; Ephesians 6:1-4*

VaDonna Jean Leaf is a free-lance writer in Stratford, Iowa. Reprinted by permission from *Christian Herald*.

2

A Day in Divorce Court

> The judge asks the woman
> if the couple can reconcile.
> The woman looks at her husband,
> then sobs, "No, sir."

by Miller Clarke

I'VE ATTENDED many weddings over the years—of relatives, friends, fellow church members. But I've never been to a divorce before today.

I ask a sheriff's deputy in the courthouse hallway where the divorce court is. She points me to a nearby bulletin board, where I find the names of several judges. Under each name hangs a stapled sheaf of papers listing the cases scheduled in that judge's court. One quick look at his docket and you can see who's presiding in divorce court; he's the judge with cases tellingly listed as *Jones v. Jones, Moroni v. Moroni, Gonzales v. Gonzales, Adams v. Adams,* and so on. Too many to count quickly. So I note the room number and ask the deputy where to find room G-3.

The basement hallway outside the door marked G-3 is beginning to fill up a half hour before the court opens its daily session. As I take a seat on one of the pewlike benches lining the hall and observe the growing crowd waiting for the court-room door to open, I'm suddenly struck by the realization that unlike a wedding where the identities of a bride and groom are obvious, it's a lot harder to spot the principals at a divorce.

Small clusters of people seem to be deliberately avoiding eye contact with other little clusters. Some people evidently have friends or family along for support. Yet other men and several women seem to be alone. Lawyers bustle up and down the corridor, huddling with each other and sometimes carry-ing on hushed conversations with their clients. The lawyers are easy to spot; they're the ones in nice suits, carrying brief-cases or legal files. But I can't begin to guess who's divorcing whom.

Looking around, I see a few smiles. Reassuring ones from the lawyers, forced ones from their clients. I can sense the heaviness—a tangibly somber air. It feels like the air in a hospital waiting room or a funeral home.

Finally the door to the courtroom opens, and the lawyers disappear inside. Everyone else waits, so I stay in the hall with them. Ten minutes pass. A handful of new lawyers go into court, a couple of others slip out.

Franklin v. Franklin

The next time a lawyer opens the door and walks into the courtroom, I follow him and squeeze into the last bench in the back of what seems an extremely cramped room. A dozen lawyers fill almost all the available seating as Judge Williams lists the cases in the order he will hear them. Then he calls the first case: *Franklin v. Franklin.*

The bailiff steps into the hall to announce the case and is followed back into the courtroom by a couple in their early

20s. At her lawyer's direction, Mrs. Franklin steps to the witness chair next to the judge's bench and is sworn in. Her husband sits in a straight chair less than six feet away as the judge asks her name and address and makes sure she's been a resident of the county for six months.

The judge pages through the open file in front of him, stopping from time to time to ask brief questions:

"How long have you been married, Ms. Franklin?"

"Four years."

"And you have one child born of this marriage?"

She sniffles. "Yes, sir."

"And he's two years old?"

"That's right."

"You understand and consent to the divorce agreement your lawyer prepared for you?"

"Yes, sir." Her voice cracks. "I do." Tears are trickling down her face.

The judge sets down the papers and says in a kindly voice, "Ms. Franklin, if you would like to postpone this proceeding until 30 days from now, I'd be glad to wait. If you think there's any chance you and your husband can reconcile your differences. Do you want to do that, or do you want to proceed?"

She's crying now as she answers. The only word I can make out is "proceed."

The judge looks reluctant, but the woman's lawyer speaks up. "Your Honor, I don't know if you remember or not, but this case was originally scheduled 30 days ago, and I asked that it be put off because I didn't think Ms. Franklin was ready. But she hasn't reconsidered."

The judge studies the woman for a moment and then

asks, "All right then, are you willing to testify that the differences between you are irreconcilable?"

She takes a deep breath. "Yes, sir." Her voice is stronger.

The judge turns his attention to the husband. "And how do you feel about this, Mr. Franklin?"

"I don't like it!"

"You understand that in this state if one party declares that the differences are irreconcilable, I have no choice but to grant a divorce."

The man nods sullenly.

The judge turns again to Mrs. Franklin. "There's no chance the two of you can work out your differences?" She glances at her husband and then looks back to the judge as she sobs, "No, sir."

I feel like a voyeur looking through a window at a world of private pain. Except this couple's anguish is being dragged out before a roomful of people. I wonder if the judge, the court recorder, and the lawyers in the room feel as uncomfortable as I do. Probably not. They work amid such raw emotion every day.

The judge peruses the papers one more time. "If I grant you joint custody of your son, will the two of you be able to work out a reasonable visitation agreement?"

Mrs. Franklin chokes out one more "Yes, sir." Her husband nods again.

"Then I'll sign the papers. You are now divorced. And you can go."

The man jumps to his feet and bolts for the door without a word to his lawyer or anyone else. He passes me with his teeth clenched and his eyes staring straight ahead. His ex-wife pauses for a few seconds to confer with her lawyer before she walks past me, dabbing at her eyes with a wadded-up tissue and fighting to stifle her sobs. Their entire divorce proceeding lasted less than 10 minutes.

Miller v. Miller

The bailiff calls the next couple, *Miller v. Miller*, in from the hallway, and the judge goes through the same procedure. This couple has been married for 32 years, and the youngest of their six children has just turned 21. Evidently a settlement has been agreed to with nothing being contested.

"I assume you want to keep your married name rather than go back to your maiden name," the judge finally says to Mrs. Miller.

"Uh . . . I don't know." She seems surprised at the question.

The judge tries to help. "You've been Mrs. Miller most of your life. All your children are Millers. Wouldn't it be better to keep the name?"

"I guess so," she responds.

"OK, then," the judge says as he signs the document. "Your divorce is now final."

The Millers leave the courtroom one at a time, neither showing any visible emotion. Their case took even less time than the Franklins'—32 years of marriage terminates in a seven-minute legal procedure.

Two more uncontested divorces follow and are disposed of in short order. Then comes a woman in her 40s whose husband isn't present; he isn't even represented by a lawyer. The woman testifies she was married less than eight months ago and has been separated for more than three months. She has a daughter from a previous marriage. Her lawyer presents the judge with her request and rationale for her husband to make a cash settlement to pay his share of two sizable loans she took out during their marriage to finance his truck, a new stereo system, and a $1,500 diamond ring he bought for himself. The judge quickly looks over her request, the loan documentation, and several bills of sale before he grants her request and signs her divorce papers.

Another couple is called. Again it all seems cut and dried. The only real question the judge has pertains to the amount of the man's child-support payments. But his wife's lawyer says, "They're right within the written guidelines, Your Honor." The man's lawyer agrees. "OK then," Judge Williams says, "I'll grant this divorce. You may go."

The couple leaves with no real show of emotion. It's as if they are numb, or perhaps all their feelings have long since been spent.

A Death That Never Ends

In less than three hours, I've witnessed the dissolution of six marriages. But what's even more sobering is the realization of all I *haven't* seen. These sad stories didn't start here, but neither do they end here. Six new divorces are now final. However, the effects of these divorces have not and never will be finalized.

I remember the words of a teenager I once interviewed about her parents' divorce. She told me she'd heard people compare divorce to a death. "But I think it's worse," she said. "Because death is a onetime event. You grieve and life goes on. But the death is over. It's in the past. A divorce just goes on forever."

I think of an adult friend whose father recently divorced her mother and married her mother's best friend. "Now I know what it must be like for people who lose their entire families in a plane crash," she says. "Oh sure, my parents and my brothers and sisters are all alive, but we can never be together again. I've lost my family forever. It's gone!"

I think, too, of other divorces that have touched my life recently. I recall the hundreds of hours my wife and I have spent in the last five years on long-distance telephone conversations with my sister-in-law in the wake of a messy, ugly divorce.

I think of friends separated from their own children by hundreds, even thousands of miles—people whose parental relationships are now limited to long-distance phone calls, alternate holidays, and two weeks every summer.

But I'm not sure that's any worse than the case of the couple at my church who got divorced last year. Our new congregational directory includes two pictures of their family. One shows him with their teenage son and six-year-old daughter. Right beside it a photo shows his ex-wife with the same two children. Every time I open the church directory I cringe at those pictures and what they so painfully symbolize.

Divorce is always more complicated, always more painful than the simple legal proceedings that went on in courtroom G-3. My knowing that made my morning in divorce court extremely depressing. It's good that we all go to more weddings than divorces. Yet a morning in divorce court wouldn't be a bad idea for anyone.

Attending a wedding can be a reminder of our marriage vows. But a visit to divorce court can also serve as a valuable warning. For me it was a sober reminder of the stakes and of the challenges all our marriages face.

BACKGROUND SCRIPTURE: Matthew 19:3-9; I Corinthians 7:10-15

Miller Clarke is a pseudonym used to protect the identity of some people mentioned in this chapter.

3

My Brother, the Alcoholic and Drug Abuser

When he asked if he could come home, his wife said it would be crowded with three in the bed.

by Stephen M. Miller

MY YOUNGER BROTHER took his eight-shot revolver and loaded it with two bullets placed four chambers apart. Then he spun the cylinder. In the game he played, Russian roulette, he would have one chance in four of taking a bullet to the head with the first shot.

My 32-year-old brother, an alcoholic and drug user, decided on this game a few days after he failed to patch up his marriage. He wanted to return to the wife and two small children he had left several months before.

He had gone to his wife's apartment and had talked with her in the doorway.

"I told her I wanted to stay," he confided to me. "She looked at me and smiled and said, 'Well, it'll be kind of crowded, seeing how there's somebody else in the bed right now.'"

That's when he realized there was no going back.

He put the gun to the right side of his head and pulled the trigger. It didn't fire.

As he sat in an old chair in his tiny living room, the television played its scenes: "Wheel of Fortune," of all shows. Without spinning the cylinder, he pulled the trigger again. Nothing.

If the next chamber was empty, the fourth would certainly not be. Again without spinning the cylinder, he pulled the trigger. Again, nothing.

The fourth time would certainly kill him. He knew he was really going to die. But he wanted to die. He figured hell could not be worse than his life. He put the gun to his head. By now tears were streaming down his face. He pulled the trigger.

Nothing.

In deep rage he flung open the cylinder and saw that the third attempt had been a hit. But it hadn't fired. He slammed the cylinder closed again, spun it around, and shot at the wall. A slug ripped through the plasterboard and sank deep into the wood.

"I remember sitting there thinking," he said, "I can't even kill myself right."

The Bent Arrow

When we were growing up, I thought we were a living version of the idealistic Walton family of TV fame. The folks at church even called me John Boy because I liked writing and was the oldest of the five children. But alongside the four straight arrows flew Chuck, the bent arrow.

"He was the one we had trouble keeping a handle on," Mom said. "His friends were absolutely opposite of our own family. Sometimes I wondered if we were as close as I thought we were. I wondered what would draw him to the lowest . . ." Her voiced trailed into silence.

Chuck was in fifth grade when he first got drunk. He and Tom, one of the bullies of the grade school, skipped class for the occasion.

Tom's dad was an alcoholic. "Tom drank," Chuck said, "because when he'd come home, his dad would beat him; and he figured if he got drunk, he wouldn't feel the pain as bad."

A cousin of Tom called the two off sick. And the boys took a six-pack of Pabst Blue Ribbon beer and hiked half a mile to the woods-shrouded cemetery in the suburbs of Akron, Ohio. Out front was an empty fountain. The two climbed inside, for protection from the cool spring winds.

"That was the first time I ever drank and really got drunk," Chuck said. "I got sick. I remember the taste of it. It smelled and tasted like ear wax. It was terrible. I don't know why I drank it. I guess to get the buzz or to be like Tom. I don't know, maybe to fit in. It seemed like a lot of people did it."

Mom had been praying and fasting for Chuck since his young teens. She hadn't known his drug problem began this early—when he was 10 years old. When I told her, she sat silently for a while. Then I asked her what she was thinking.

"That's the age of his son," she whispered.

When I asked her if she felt guilty about not figuring out Chuck's secret earlier, she gently asked a painful question in response. "Do you? You slept in the same room with him."

Then I asked Mom how she felt about four of her children staying in the church and one slipping into drugs. She said, "It made me feel like it could happen in any family."

By the time Chuck was in 10th grade, he was smoking marijuana with his school friends. Then a couple of years later, in the army at Fort Bragg, N.C., he began drinking heavier and experimenting with other drugs. He said he tried everything from sucking dried LSD drops off slips of paper to eating hallucinogenic mushrooms that grew beside cow manure.

"Whenever I went to the ammo dump, I always scarfed up a lot of mushrooms for the guys in my squad," he said. "Just about everybody used drugs. Everybody partied. Not just the alcohol.

"The mushrooms tasted really bitter, nasty. But next thing I knew, I was down on the ground staring at grass. You needed to be outside with a lot of room, because you always got a closed-in feeling."

When his military stint ended, he returned to his hometown with a wife and a son. He also stopped the experimenting. He limited himself to alcohol and marijuana. But even with that, he said knew he had a problem.

"I remember Dad came over," Chuck said. "I had just gotten done smoking a joint. I had a real bad hangover from the night before. He came up, and he was talking to Barbara and wanting to know where I was. She told him I was with a friend or something. And all the time I was in the back bedroom hiding because I was ashamed, and I didn't want him to find me and see me. That was eight years ago; I knew I had a problem back then."

He tried to quit, partly because of Dad. But three weeks was the longest Chuck managed to stay off the alcohol.

When his marriage collapsed, he sought help by returning to the church of his childhood. All of our family still attended there except me; I had moved out of state. Then one

Sunday Chuck overheard two ushers talking in the hallway just outside the sanctuary.

"They were talking about me leaving such a good-looking woman and giving up my family and coming back to church, sitting in there, thinking everything was hunky-dory," Chuck said. "They didn't know I was there at the time. When I came out, they knew I had heard them. And it didn't matter."

My brother has never returned to the church.

He next sought relief in more drugs. The relief became a vicious, devouring cycle.

"In the mornings I always ate a hit of speed and had some coffee to kick me in. A few hours later I'd take my work break; I'd go to the truck and roll myself a joint to help my hangover headache. Around lunchtime I'd go to the truck and do myself up a little line of cocaine to make me feel better and give me energy.

"After work I'd go back to the herb, and then I'd crack my fifth [whiskey]. In the evenings I'd hit the bars, and I'd be doing all of it except the speed."

These were expensive habits for a factory worker who mixed plastics for a living. Chuck said he got behind in every bill. To help pay for the drugs, he sold some to his friends and coworkers, acting as a go-between for the Jamaica-supplied dealer he bought from. For this, the dealer rewarded him with some free drugs. Even so he still spent about $1,500 a month on drugs, nearly $1,000 of it going for cocaine.

I asked him where he got the speed. These are prescription drugs used to control weight. He said he got them from a diet doctor in the area.

"You're not fat," I replied.

"I know."

"You're skinny." He was about 6 feet 1 inch, 160 pounds.
"I know."

"How did you get them from him?"

"I'd just go in there and tell him I needed to lose some weight."

"Did he know what was going on?"

"Sure he knew. [A friend of mine] was getting speed from him too. And she weighs 108 pounds."

Every other week Chuck would go to the doctor for 30 "beans." The pills cost about $1.00 apiece. And until Chuck became deeply addicted to them, he often sold some to others for $5.00 apiece.

"It got to the place where I quit selling them. I just enjoyed doing them so much. Then I'd have to drink at night to be able to pass out. I'd wake up in the wee hours of the morning and go downstairs to make another drink so that I could go back to sleep."

No one in the family knew Chuck was using drugs this heavily. Not even his work buddies knew. Mom and I knew he drank and figured he used some "light" drugs on occasion. I was naive enough to think he took them as I took candy. I had no idea of the inner battle he waged with these powerful chemicals.

Solo Detox

My brother decided to stop all drugs the Sunday afternoon his ex-wife and her new husband came to pick up the kids. Chuck had spent the weekend with his 10-year-old son and 4-year-old daughter. Chuck told me the couple tried to sell him marijuana in front of the children.

"I never, I never did anything when I had my kids! I ended up kicking them out of the house."

But as he sat there alone, he said he realized he was no better than they were. Just more secretive. That's when he scraped up every drug he could find and flushed it all.

"I poured my whiskey down the john. I dumped out a gram and a half of coke [enough for six uses]. I dumped my speed out, and I dumped all my herb. I flushed it. I stood there and watched it go down. And, like a fool, I thought that would be the end of it."

He said he felt good about what he did. And though he couldn't get any sleep that night, he thought a hard day of work the next day would leave him exhausted enough to sleep.

Instead, a day away from drugs left him with a desperate craving and in the first stages of withdrawal.

"I remember that Monday after work. I literally ran in my house. I cracked the door getting in, I was in such a hurry. I beelined it to the bathroom, hoping I had dropped something. I remember cussing myself out standing in front of the john, and crying because I flushed everything I had."

By Wednesday he knew he needed help.

At work he pulled aside the leader of his unit and told him he was going through withdrawal and that after his weekend with the kids he planned to admit himself to a hospital that treats alcoholics and drug abusers.

After work Chuck went to Mom and Dad's to wash some laundry. His eyes were red from crying. His body trembled. It was obvious to Mom something was terribly wrong.

She asked.

"Nothing's wrong," Chuck replied. "I've just got some things on my mind." He turned and looked out the door.

She stepped up behind him, rested her hand on his shoulder, and asked again.

"I just started crying. I told her, 'Mom, I'm going to have to go away for a while. I'm having withdrawal really bad right now.'

"She cried a little bit, then said, 'You want Dad and me to take you to the hospital?' I told her no, I had to wait until after the weekend. I get the kids. She said, 'You're not going to be any good to them, not like this. We'll take care of them.'"

Thursday was payday. And Chuck said he suddenly realized if he didn't get help before then, he would use the money to buy drugs to stop the roaring beneath his skin.

For a ride to the hospital he called his friend, Ron, a former alcoholic and drug abuser who had gone through detox more than a year earlier and who had remained clean, with the help of Alcoholics Anonymous.

While Chuck made the call, Mom went in the living room to tell Dad. Dad, still weak from the effects of radiation treatment in a bout with cancer, sat quietly in the recliner while Mom broke the news.

"His face turned white," Mom said. "His look was like it was the end of the road. I said, 'Dad, don't feel like that. I've been praying for this for a long time.'"

Chuck sat in the kitchen, too ashamed to face his dad. Mom came out to her boy. "She said, 'Tell your dad you love him and that everything will be OK,'" Chuck said. "And I went in. Dad had a tear coming down his face. And I reached over and gave him a hug. I told him, 'Dad, I'm sorry. I will be OK. You pray for me. Next time you see me I'll be straight.'"

Weeks before, Chuck had started attending another church in the area—the church another brother of ours had started attending. Chuck told me he knew he needed help, and he needed to be around good people. He told the pastor of his problem. And though the pastor was genuinely concerned and supportive, he was at a loss for words. He said he would pray for my brother.

As Chuck left for a month-long stay in the hospital, he asked Mom to have our brother pass along a message to the pastor. "Tell the preacher I haven't given up. I'll be back."

Mom said she stared out the door long after her boy and his friend had left. In those moments a verse of the Bible tumbled out of her memory. Psalm 138:8. "The Lord will perfect that which concerneth me" (KJV).

Detox in the Hospital

Chuck spent a sleepless night in his room with two other addicts.

Mom tossed and turned as well. "You'd think I would have prayed that God would make it easy on him," she said. "But I asked the Lord to make it hard enough that he'll always remember it and not want to go back to it again."

For 5 days Chuck fought the pangs of withdrawal in detox. It would have taken longer except he had started his own detox several days before. During the remainder of his 28 days in the hospital he kept busy with counseling, group discussion, education films on the effects of drugs, and meetings of support groups such as Alcoholics Anonymous and Narcotics Anonymous.

He said his most haunting memory during that time was on his first Sunday there. Sunday is family day. It's the only day friends and family can visit. He wasn't ready to see his children, but he watched as the family of a fellow patient arrived.

"He had a little girl, about 11, and a little boy who couldn't have been 7. I remember the boy. He picked the boy up. And the boy was hugging and kissing him and asked his dad, 'Daddy, let me smell your breath.' The boy just wanted to see if his dad was clean.

"When it was time to go, I remember the little boy just clinging to his dad. And then the boy started crying. They had to pry his fingers loose. Then the little girl said, 'Dad, we'll be here when you get out. And then we can start over.'"

That night Chuck went to the bathroom long after the lights were out. In there, crying, was the father. Chuck talked with the man. He said, "You got a chance to get your family back. All the pain you put them through, they're still there for you."

A Weekend with My Brother

My brother is out of the hospital now. He has been clean for several months. Instead of going to bars after work and on weekends, he goes to hour-long AA meetings scattered throughout Akron, where AA was born in 1935. He goes every day. He doesn't expect to need this much support forever. But he needs it now. Sometimes he goes to two meetings each day on weekends.

When I visited Chuck recently, he asked if I wanted to go to one of the meetings with him. I went to two. The most memorable was the one at Edwin Shaw Hospital, where my brother had been treated.

There were about 50 of us in the hospital cafeteria. All kinds of people. Huge, bearded biker types. Well-dressed executive types. There was a woman in her mid-20s with a little boy she kept hugging and kissing. At the table in front of us sat a frail young lady who became addicted to cough medicine. My brother told me she thought if she limited herself to cough medicine, she wouldn't become an alcoholic.

A good-looking, well-dressed, nervous young woman

was the speaker for the evening. "Hi. I'm Jill. I'm an alcoholic. For those of you who care to, help me by joining in the Serenity Prayer." Together we recited: "God grant me the serenity to accept the things I cannot change, courage to change the things I can, and wisdom to know the difference."

For 45 minutes she told the story of her plunge into alcohol. Afterward, the floor was open for comments.

A dark-haired woman in her 50s stood. She was Jill's sponsor—a fellow alcoholic assigned to encourage and help another. Among the few words she spoke were these, which continue to haunt me: "All of you in this room are my friends. You're all the friends I have."

I felt so ashamed. I've been in the church all my life. I work as an editor in my denomination. I believe God put the church here to help hurting people. Yet I had allowed ignorance to isolate me from the deep pain of alcoholics and drug abusers. My brother included.

The room was full of cigarette smoke. Nearly everyone smoked. I hate smoke. I stay away from smoking sections on planes and in restaurants. But an unearthly thing happened to me during that hour. I enjoyed the smoke. As I sat there, I knew it was saturating my hair and clothes. When I would leave the hospital, the smell would leave with me.

But I felt like I was in the Temple of God when the priests burned their incense in the sanctuary, and it wafted upward to became a fragrant offering to God. I felt like this was a holy place because I was where I was supposed to be, and Jesus was there with me, walking around the room, healing people in pain.

The meeting was nearly over when, in the back corner of the room, a thin and trembling black woman rose. She wore the blue hospital blouse of a patient. She must have been in her late 20s or early 30s. Her curly, shoulder-length hair was greased and pulled back tight off her forehead and released in a fray behind her head. The hair looked like it had been styled by the wind during a motorcycle ride. I thought then the woman looked like the stereotype of a junkie.

"I'm an alcoholic," she said. "I'm in withdrawal now."

The words broke her voice, and she began to talk between gentle sobs.

"This is the first time I've admitted I'm an alcoholic. I'm hoping and praying God will help me. Please pray for me."

My outward composure only hinted of the bitter weeping that exploded inside me. I wept for her. And for my brother, who had stood in her place two months earlier. And for myself, because I didn't know how to help.

In the closing ritual, common to most AA meetings, we all stood, joined hands, repeated the Lord's Prayer, then ended in unison, "Keep coming back."

My brother told me to wait a minute, and he walked toward the trembling woman. I followed behind.

He whispered words I could not hear. He told me later he had said he'd been through the same thing and that he had some bad days but that it gets better. Then he hugged this physically unattractive total stranger.

He stepped aside, and suddenly there I stood before her. No longer isolated from hurting people by a sanctuary, religious rites, or the fence around my suburban yard. There was just me—the never-rebellious, lifelong churchgoer—standing face-to-face before an alcoholic in the agony of withdrawal. I saw weariness in her face, a pleading in her eyes, and tears pumping down her cheeks.

She rested her hands on my back as I held her, and she laid her head on the nape of my neck.

"I'll be praying for you," I whispered.

"Thank you," she replied.

I patted her back, walked away, and carried with me on the left side of my face a sprinkling of her teardrops.

As my brother and I walked to his pickup, he smiled at me, happy I had come with him. I was happy too. For I felt I had been to a church Jesus attends.

Later that weekend, I asked Chuck how he felt about his future.

"My biggest goal is to be average. I want to be like everybody else. I want to be able to deal with my problems without drinkin' and druggin'. I want to be able to watch my kids grow up. I want to be there for my family."

I asked our mom how she feels about Chuck's future.

Her face took on a distant look, perhaps the very same one that day my brother pulled out of the driveway and left for the hospital. "The Lord will perfect that which concerneth me," she said. Then she smiled.

* * *

February 1, 1989, is Chuck's sobriety date. Of the 13 people who went through detox together at Edwin Shaw Hospital (8 men, 5 women) Chuck is the only one still drug-free. Only 1 out of 36 who take the treatment stays clean. Chuck has married a recovering alcoholic who has been drug-free nearly as long as he has been.

BACKGROUND SCRIPTURE: Psalm 138:1-8

Stephen M. Miller is editor of the Dialog Series of books and lives in Belton, Mo.

4

Why I'm Not Obsessed with Looking Attractive

Got a weight problem,
bald spot, wide nose, crooked teeth?
Welcome to the human race.

by Leola Floren Gee

I WILL ALWAYS REMEMBER the day I saw Francis Schaeffer in his underwear.

For those of you unfamiliar with the late author of such scholarly works as *Genesis in Space and Time* and *The Church at the End of the 20th Century,* Dr. Schaeffer is respected by many as a brilliant theologian, whose classically reasoned arguments for the faith remain staples in evangelical libraries.

Back in 1979 he and his wife, Edith, were in Detroit for several speaking engagements. Since I was a feature writer for one of the city's daily newspapers, I arranged to interview Mrs. Schaeffer, who is herself an accomplished author.

After introductions in their hotel suite, Dr. Schaeffer retired to the sleeping area while Mrs. Schaeffer and I settled in

35

front of a window with a view of the Detroit River and the skyline of Windsor, Ont. She poured tea, and we talked about current projects and their home in Switzerland.

Midway through our conversation the phone rang. Dr. Schaeffer answered it in the bedroom. Moments later he called to his wife, but she was busy—with the tea, I suppose—and asked if I would mind seeing what he wanted.

Leaving my notebook on the chair, I walked across the sitting room, rapped on the bedroom door, and when he said, "Come in!" I flung it open. There he stood, awash in a flood of astonishment.

Startled as he was, he managed to convey the message, and I delivered it to Mrs. Schaeffer without additional comment.

Now and forevermore, when I pick up an essay penned by that greatly admired Christian scholar, I can't help but glimpse a flashback to a bewildered, silver-haired gentleman with a telephone receiver in his hand, clad in the uniform favored by male models in JCPenney underwear ads.

No doubt about it—in our society, appearances count. Our weight, body shape, posture, and makeup (or lack of it), the way we dress (or don't dress), and the manner in which we wear our hair all telegraph messages to the people we meet. It may not be fair, given the fact that underneath we're all pretty much the same, but it's a fact of life that others often evaluate our worth based solely on the way we look.

Obsessed About Good Looks

It's frustrating when it happens in the classroom or the workplace; it's tragic when it happens in the Christian community. True enough, maintaining a healthy diet and life-style makes good sense, but the scales are tipped way out of balance. In too many circles, the pursuit of physical fitness and attractiveness has become an acceptable obsession.

Allow me to illustrate with an example all too familiar to women today. A few years ago I attended a Tupperware party along with a dozen members of my adult Sunday School class. Tupperware parties are not usually life-changing events. But for me, this party became a turning point in my life. More than half of us had children under two years of age and were still in the process of losing "those last 10 pounds." (It goes without saying that we will still be in the process of shedding those last 10 pounds when we are grand-mothers.)

Even though no one present was significantly over-weight, the conversation turned—as it often does—to dieting. That's when one of the slimmer members of the group told of visiting a health club that routinely measures one's per-centage of body fat. She lifted her arm and pinched an inch of skin to show how the process works, while the rest of us nobly ignored the brownies, chips, pretzels, and dips spread out like a Roman feast on the coffee table.

Nobody had the nerve to eat anything after that, and the dismayed and embarrassed hostess sent us home with doggie bags filled with leftovers to feed to our husbands and kids (and which, no doubt, several of us devoured at the first red traffic signal).

This little party was a turning point for me because it was here I started keeping mental notes on what I'm convinced is an unhealthy preoccupation with weight and good looks in the Christian community. Here's a sampling of my obser-vations.

• A Bible study leader became pregnant five months be-fore she was scheduled to stand up at a relative's wedding. She nearly starved herself during those first critical weeks of her baby's development, because she was bound and determined not to forfeit the deposit on her bridesmaid dress, and she wanted a flat stomach in wedding photos.

• A nationwide Christian organization maintains a weight requirement for its leadership. Though the policy is not widely publicized, women judged overweight are not considered for leadership roles, the theory being that they should set a good example by exhibiting self-control.

• Two teenage girls in a senior high youth group frequently agonize over which crash diets to try. One of the girls has diabetes, and the other is undergoing chemotherapy treatments for leukemia; but like many of their contemporaries, they are more concerned with appearances than lifelong health. Why? They think they'll get more dates if they're thin. (And they probably will.) It should come as no surprise that Christians are not exempt from eating disorders such as anorexia and bulimia.

• Then there's a woman I'll call Cheryl. She's in her early 40s, divorced, and the mother of seven. During the first year or so that I knew her, whenever we ran into each other at church, she made disparaging remarks concerning her weight. Obviously her appearance bothered her a great deal, but I kept the conversations as upbeat as possible, joking about our mutual emotional attachment to chocolate.

Much later I found out that Cheryl had left her husband after years of physical abuse, and though I talked with her many times in church, it wasn't until recently I learned that when she went home, it was to a shelter for battered women.

Cheryl's problems were deeper and much more serious than a weakness for M&Ms, but it is less threatening to talk about physical weight loss or gain than spiritual loss or gain.

Besides, it doesn't require as extensive an investment in time and energy. If Cheryl and I could keep our relationship at a superficial level in which the most personal subject we discussed was "those last 10 pounds," we were both more comfortable.

Unfortunately, the last time I checked, "comfort" wasn't listed among the fruits of the Spirit.

If our relationships with fellow believers never progress beyond discussions of hairstyles and hemlines, how can we possibly follow the biblical mandate to build up the Body of Christ? At the least, our preoccupation with physical appearance wastes time and energy; at its worst, it can blind us to the devastating problems of others.

Overcoming the Obsession

Margie was a stylish but plump woman in her 30s, whose carbonated personality always bubbled over into laughter. A fashion writer, she frequently traveled to New York or Europe, sometimes for weeks at a stretch, so no one was very concerned when she was gone for a couple of months.

When she finally returned, she looked as if her head had been transplanted onto the body of a Los Angeles Laker cheerleader. She was thin and gorgeous in a turquoise knit dress and broadbrim hat. Coworkers raved about how great she looked. She smiled and said very little.

That's the last time we saw her, because within a matter of weeks, she died of lung cancer. In those final, sad days of her life, I wish I had spent less time looking at her clothes and more time looking into her eyes. She needed friends, not an audience, and in that respect we let her down.

Christians, of all people, should look beyond the hair, the

makeup, the clothes, and the body type. We need to look at the person's spirit—and the need—within. Only in doing this can we "carry each other's burdens, and in this way you will fulfill the law of Christ" (Galatians 6:2).

I like what author and pastor Charles Swindoll has to say in *The Grace Awakening:* "It was never God's intention for all His children to look alike or embrace identical life-styles." And yet so much of our effort goes into conforming to an unwritten code of dress and appearance, that we can look at people day after day, year after year, without seeing the human being beneath the uniform.

If we're ever to see one another as God sees us, we need to shift the emphasis away from physical attributes and focus instead on qualities of lasting value. When we meet a kindergarten child in the church hallway, do we admire her dress and tell her how cute she looks? Or do we say, "Boy, that was great the way you shared your crayons today"? If a teen in the youth group slows down long enough for us to have a conversation, do we tell him what swell taste he has in shirts? Or do we let him know that we noticed the friendly way he introduced himself to a visitor?

I once pulled aside one of my daughter's favorite Sunday School teachers and told him how much I appreciated his positive attitude and willingness to serve in that area of our church family. His eyes brightened as he told me how great it feels when the children greet him with hugs at the beginning of class. I'd never have gotten that response by complimenting him on his choice in neckties.

I have to admit, I might not have bothered to thank him for his work if it hadn't been for a kind stranger who once took the trouble to congratulate me for keeping my cool when my then three-year-old kiddie terrorist dumped her drink on the floor in Wendy's. It may not sound like much, but a few words of affirmation to a tired mom meant more than a dozen casual compliments on a new dress or hairstyle.

After all, a compliment on my hair means the woman who cuts it is doing a good job. A compliment on my controlled temper, however, means that God is indeed answering my prayer for parental patience. It also means that the next time the cup tips over, I'll be more likely to respond in a loving manner, and thus bear witness to a life transformed by Christ. Best of all, the object of this witness will be the most precious audience in the world to me, my own child.

Granted, identifying and acknowledging godly qualities in those with whom we live and worship requires more effort than the casual "nice dress" and "new suit, huh?" type of compliment. But our family and friends are worth it, aren't they?

Beyond "Wow, Can You Accessorize!"

A mother I know told me about a conversation she had with her son when he was in first grade. It seems his teacher, whom he greatly admired, went on a weight-loss program and then told the class about her progress. When the boy came home from school, he asked, "Mom, shouldn't you lose some weight?"

Rather than responding out of hurt or annoyance, she replied, "Well, let's think about this, Honey. Which would you rather have, a mother who spends a lot of time on her hair, her makeup, and her appearance, and doesn't pay a whole lot of attention to you? Or a mother who maybe weighs a little more than she should but always has plenty of time for you?"

The choice was easy, even for a first grader.

Got a weight problem? Bald spot? Skinny arms? Thick

ankles? Ugly knees? Wide nose? Crooked teeth? Elephant ears? Limp hair? Oily skin? Dry skin? Birthmark? Oily-dry-flaky skin? Hangnails? Love handles? Two chins? Droopy eyelids? Freckles? Wrinkles? Split ends?

Welcome to the human race.

Nobody's perfect, and as long as we keep comparing ourselves with each other—or worse, airbrushed magazine photos—we'll drive ourselves crazy.

If your physical imperfection is related to a health problem, seek medical help, and counseling if necessary. But if it's strictly cosmetic, ask yourself this question: 100 years from now, how much will it matter?

One hundred years from now, will it matter how faithfully you studied your Bible, how often you took time to meditate on God's attributes, and whether you were available to drive a neighbor to the doctor, or listen to a troubled child or a depressed coworker? If it will matter 100 years from now, then it matters today.

On the other hand, 100 years from now, will it matter that your slacks were always neatly pressed, and your eyebrows symmetrical? Will it matter whether you lived and died a size 8, or a size 14? Will anyone walk up to you in heaven and say, "Wow, it always blessed my heart the way you could accessorize"?

Humans look on the outward appearance and long to see a nice outfit on a trim figure. God looks on the heart and sees eternal consequences. Which one needs glasses?

BACKGROUND SCRIPTURE: *I Samuel 16:7; Galatians 6:2; I Peter 3:3-4*

Leola Floren Gee is a Nazarene free-lance writer and a newspaper columnist. She lives with her husband and two children in Novi, Mich.

5

The Bride Who Moved to a Pig Farm

> *"Do you have any idea
> what it's like
> to crawl into bed with a man
> who smells like a hog?"*

by Craig Massey

JEANETTE sat at her desk in the living room and looked out the window at thousands of greening acres bathed in the May sunlight.

To the left, the cherry orchard stood in full bloom. Closer at hand lay Bluff, the collie, stretched out near the clothesline. Her three pups were playing a game of ragtag.

To the right was the barn. Jeanette rose and slammed shut the two open windows. "I've got to tell someone," she whispered angrily.

Returning to her desk, she grabbed a pen and her note pad. "Dear Carol," she wrote fiercely. "Hogs, swine, boars, sows, piglets, shoats, and porkers . . . do you know what those creatures do? They smell and they make crude noises.

"If it weren't so horrible, it would be funny. Here I am on the outskirts of Northfield, a town of 200, living with a husband who is nursemaid to 1,500 of those things. This would be a beautiful spring day, but the wind is from the southwest, and pigs foul the air. I just closed the windows to escape the pig punishment.

"How did I, a girl from a Chicago suburb, ever get conned into marrying an ag major from Boondock, U.S.A.? A new lot of feeder pigs came in this week, and Herb's out there now doing something to them. For 15 hours yesterday he was out there doing something to them. He was so tired last night that he collapsed in bed after he ate and fell asleep in a minute—and without a bath!

"Do you have any idea what it's like to be married six months less a day and have to crawl into bed with a man who smells like a hog and who, when he snores, sounds like one?

"I called my mother this morning and told her about it. All she did was laugh. 'You knew he was a pig farmer when you married him,' she said. I was absolutely furious!

"Here I am, with qualifications for teaching high school math, and what am I doing? Picking up socks and pants and shirts that smell like pigs. Living in a house that smells like pigs. And loving a husband who smells like pigs. I keep telling myself, 'I do believe the Lord brought Herb and me together, but did the Lord bring me and the pigs together?' "

Although Jeanette finished the letter in a lighter tone, as she sealed the envelope she stared at the barn again and wrinkled her nose. Then she went to the freezer, pulled out a package marked "Select Pork Loin Chops," and tossed it on the kitchen table. "How can civilized people eat meat that looks like pigs and smells like pigs?" she said aloud, laughing in spite of herself.

She thawed the package in the microwave and continued her housework. Herb called at 5:00 on the intercom from the barn. "Honey, I'll be in in about an hour."

A Hug from Pigman

True to his word, he swung open the screen door that led to the kitchen and engulfed Jeanette in his arms. She held her breath as his lips found hers. "What a day! What a day!" he exclaimed. "Spring is busting out all over!"

Into the wash goes my blouse, Jeanette thought. That's the third time this week.

As Herb headed for the sink to wash, Jeanette watched his mud-stained boots leave marks on the newly scrubbed linoleum. She thought, Why'd I waste my time?

When he finally plopped down at the table, Herb exclaimed, "Hey, pork chops—hooray!" After returning thanks, he reached for the platter. "This is one good lot of shoats."

"Maybe you should have married Miss Piggy," Jeanette said, forcing a laugh.

Herb reached over and touched his wife's nose. "With a cute little snout like yours, Miss Piggy never had a chance."

As Jeanette slid the smallest chop to her plate, she wondered, Will Mr. Pigman remember our six-month anniversary? And if he does, what will he want to do—watch the pigs wallow?

Herb studied Jeanette. "I've been pretty busy taking over the farm from Dad. There was a lot of work to be done; and, of course, when pigs arrive, there's a lot to do. It won't always be like this."

But the grunting groaners and their smells will be there, Jeanette thought, and as soon as these are gone, there'll be another lot.

"I have a couple hours' work to do," Herb said when he had finished eating.

Jeanette cleaned up the kitchen, threw some clothes in the washer, and turned on the television. I'm bored, she thought, and lonely.

The farmhouse had been in the family for 150 years. Herb's parents had turned it over to him when they retired to Florida the day after the wedding. Jeanette, always interested in antiques, was fascinated with the furnishings. Herb's ancestors had made most of the items by hand out of cherry wood cut from the orchard.

At 8:30 Herb called on the intercom. "Sorry, honey, but I have two more hours' work."

Jeanette took a shower and went to bed at 10:30. She heard Herb come in and make a phone call, and then was relieved to hear the shower downstairs.

The following morning a spring rain swept up from the southwest. A mist hung over the countryside, blanketing the earth with the heavy odor of pigs.

Honeymoon Part 2

Six months of swine smell, Jeanette thought. Happy anniversary!

Just then the intercom buzzed.

"Honey, I'll be up in a half hour. Dress in your best, and lay out my best too. We're off to celebrate the greatest marriage that ever took place!"

"What?" Jeanette asked.

"Ask no questions—just get ready."

When he reached the house, Herb explained. "I called up Max. He'll come over to check on the hogs the next day and a half. We have a five-hour drive to Chicago. We'll see your folks, and I've made reservations at the Hyatt for a second honeymoon weekend."

In the car that morning, Jeanette forgot the farm and soon was lost in the joys of her former environment, until they returned home Saturday evening—all too soon, she thought. Although she fought her feelings, Jeanette found herself sinking into depression.

On the following Tuesday, restless and a bit bored, she picked up her Bible and turned to the Song of Solomon. Herb had read it to her on their honeymoon night. "Tell me, O thou whom my soul loveth," she read, "where thou feedest, where thou makest thy flock to rest at noon" (1:7, KJV).

She paused, then looked at the barn and thought, I know where my beloved is, and I know where his herd is. That bride's husband didn't have swine—mine does.

Immediately, she felt embarrassed. That man may have had goats, and they smell. Maybe he had sheep—they're dumb.

She felt an urge to be with Herb. I've made myself lonely, she thought. I've separated myself from my beloved.

She rose and glanced at the clock: five minutes to 12. Impulsively, she turned off the oven where a casserole was baking. She ran upstairs, found an old blouse and a pair of blue jeans, then pulled on her old hiking shoes. Dashing downstairs, she took a deep breath, opened the door, and headed for the barn.

The odor was there, still hanging in the spring air.

She had been in the barn only once before, the day they returned from their honeymoon. Opening the door, she saw Herb with his back to her and worked her way toward him through the maze of squealing, squalling, and grunting pigs in pens. Herb wasn't aware of her presence until she rested her hand on his shoulder.

"Can I help?" she asked.

He grabbed her and kissed her. "You sure can!" he said. Then he pointed: "They all have to be inoculated." He led her to a bench and showed her how to measure the serum.

At two o'clock, Herb said, "Hey, we haven't had any lunch!"

Together they went to the house. "It would've taken me over four hours to do what we just did in two hours," Herb said.

"Would you like me to be your hired hand?" she asked with mischief in her eyes.

He stopped on the kitchen steps and kissed her. "Anytime," he said.

After lunch Jeanette said, "I'll just put these dishes in the dishwasher and clean up, and then I'll be down."

As she left the house a little later, the sun broke through the mist. Somehow the odor didn't seem as bad. When you work with them, you smell like them, she thought. My senses must be dulled.

Just before she fell asleep that night, cradled in Herb's arms, she remembered the letter she had written to Carol and never mailed. She decided then to leave it unmailed.

BACKGROUND SCRIPTURE: *Song of Songs 1:7; Ephesians 5:21-25*

Craig Massey is a family counselor and seminar lecturer. He lives with his wife in McNaughton, Wis. Massey learned of this true story by talking with Jeanette and has written the chapter with her permission.

6

Uncomfortable Encounters with the Town Drunk

A pastor's wife had little compassion until she was mistaken for a bag lady.

by Denise George

I DIDN'T WANT TO BE HERE. Sitting stiffly in a metal folding chair in the basement of the First Baptist Church of Chelsea, Mass., I could only half listen as Larry, a shaggy-headed teen-ager, read from Matthew 25.

Around me sat nine other tough-looking, blue-jeaned youth. Former drug users, alcoholics, and gang members, each one had recently accepted Christ and had joined our Friday night Bible study.

Chelsea, a poor, crowded, inner city located on the outskirts of Boston, was known for its delinquent youth, drug selling, and street violence. A shiver passed through me as I contemplated three more years here. After only a few months, I already intensely disliked this place.

As Larry read, my thoughts drifted to the lovely Georgian

pastorate we left to come here. After two years there, my husband, Timothy, had been accepted to study at Harvard Divinity School in Cambridge. He had also been called as pastor of Chelsea's small mission church.

Larry continued. "I was an hungred, and ye gave me meat: I was thirsty, and ye gave me drink: I was a stranger, and ye took me in . . . Verily I say unto you, Inasmuch as ye have done it unto one of the least of these my brethren, ye have done it unto me" (Matthew 25:35, 40, KJV).

I loved that particular scripture. Years before, my grandfather had put music to the words to help me learn them.

As I played the melody memories in my mind, suddenly the basement door burst open. A cold October wind swept into the room, wildly flipping Bible pages.

In Comes the Town Drunk

An old man staggered inside. He wore a navy blue suit 20 years out of style. He was covered with city dirt. Wisps of white hair danced around his face, a face carved by years of hard drinking and hostile New England winters.

I recognized him—the town drunk. No one knew his real name, but the street kids had dubbed him "Johnny Cornflakes" because he routinely searched trash cans looking for the last few flakes in discarded cereal boxes. Johnny lived on the streets, slept under apartment porches, and ate scraps of food tossed to him by local restaurant owners.

With stooped shoulders and an age-etched frown, he resembled a Ringling Brothers clown as he limped into the room. He proceeded to step on 12 pairs of feet only to land, amazingly, upright in the chair next to mine. Once seated, he turned his entire body toward me. With large bloodshot eyes, he gazed into my face. Even though he seemed a comical figure, a second of panic passed through me. As a young girl, I had once been frightened by a man intoxicated with strong drink. Still staring at me, Johnny opened his food-encrusted, toothless mouth and smiled.

The stench of body odor and alcohol hit me full force. I jerked my head away and wrapped my hand tightly over my face. I thought I would be sick.

How I longed at that moment to be back home with the people I knew and loved.

As I struggled hard to keep back the nausea, I remembered the first time I met Johnny. It had not been pleasant.

Two weeks before on a Sunday afternoon, Timothy and I had given our first dinner party in Chelsea for six out-of-state guests. We could only afford onion soup, baked beans, and my "sweet potato surprise," but we made the table elegant with our silver, china, and lace wedding gifts.

"Relax, Denise," Timothy told me for the 16th time.

"I just want our guests to remember this dinner for a long time," I whispered.

Thanks to Johnny Cornflakes, our guests would, indeed, remember this dinner party. For just as I served the soup, the front door flew open. And there, in all of his inebriated glory, stood Johnny Cornflakes.

With a grin and a bow, he tottered to the table. Unashamedly, he picked up the silver serving spoon and began shoveling my sweet potato surprise into his mouth. Timothy saw the horror on my face, so he filled a plate with food and gently led Johnny to the kitchen to eat.

Johnny's Twisted Foot

Vividly remembering the dinner party Johnny ruined, I turned to give Johnny an angry glare. That's when I noticed the people around me looking at Johnny's shoe. I saw it too. The twisted mass of unsocked foot, crippled by a childhood disease, stuffed into a shoe with a large, gaping hole. Johnny had pushed cardboard into the hole, trying to shut out the blustery New England northeasters.

Larry broke the uncomfortable silence. "You know, it won't be long till winter snow comes. I think Jesus would want us to buy Johnny another shoe."

The others agreed and immediately emptied their pockets. Larry counted out $15.00.

"This should be enough for a shoe," he guessed. "Let's get Johnny to the foot doctor tomorrow."

I couldn't believe my ears. They actually were going to spend their $15.00 on a shoe for Johnny!

"Well, I believe in helping the poor, but aren't there agencies that could give Johnny a shoe?" I asked.

"With all the papers and red tape," a teenager piped up, "it would be summer before Johnny got a shoe."

At that point, I decided to keep quiet.

The next day, Timothy and another church worker took Johnny to the doctor. "Johnny's foot is so badly deformed," he explained, "a new shoe designed to fit him will cost $113.92."

"There's no way we can buy that shoe at $113.92!" I told Timothy later that evening. "Johnny'll just have to live with cardboard in his shoe."

The next Friday night, we told the Bible study group the bad news.

"Since we can't buy the shoe, let's use the money for something else," I suggested.

But Larry wouldn't hear of it. "Johnny needs that shoe. Anyway," he asked, "isn't Johnny one of the 'least of these' that Jesus talks about?"

"But—"

Larry interrupted me. "We'll just have to earn the money!"

Teens Hit the Street

The next morning, 10 teenagers hit the streets of Chelsea in search of odd jobs. They picked up trash, moved furniture, and washed windows. It took them six weeks. But before the November snow came, they had earned $113.92. They bought Johnny's shoe.

It was raining the next Friday night as we admired the shoe and waited for Johnny. One hour, two hours, three hours crept by. But Johnny didn't come.

"Do you think he's left town?" someone asked.

"Maybe he's sick somewhere, or even . . . dead," another offered.

I could stand it no longer. "The old drunk!" I heard myself blurt out. "He could at least come get his shoe!"

Then Larry spoke. "Well, we'll just have to go out and find Johnny and take the shoe to him."

"But it's not safe to be on the streets this time of night," I said.

But they were determined. So I decided to tag along.

For the next few hours, we crawled under apartment porches, searched the city's trash bins, and walked the dirty, wet streets calling his name. But, no Johnny. We finally gave up and headed back to the church.

On the way back, we passed Johnny's favorite restaurant. "Let's take one more look," someone said. We walked around to the back and looked. And there, sprawled out in the alley, soaking wet and covered with mud, lay Johnny Cornflakes.

We knelt beside Johnny, and Larry tenderly pulled the new shoe onto Johnny's twisted foot. Then someone offered up a simple prayer for the old man who had spent a lifetime sprawled out in an alley.

Scraps for Me

Just then the restaurant owner came out, carrying a small plastic bag of food scraps. As he tossed them over to Johnny, he hesitated, and then he looked me square in the face. "Here, lady," he said. "There's probably enough for you too."

As he shut the door, I caught my reflection in the glass. I was shocked by what he had said and by what I now saw. There I was, kneeling in an alley beside the town drunk, my hair wet and disheveled, my clothes covered with mud. The restaurant owner had misjudged me. He couldn't see beneath the layers of city dirt to know who I really was. No one had ever spoken to me like that. An appalling thought came: He thinks I'm a bag lady.

I looked again at Johnny, who sat and stared at his new shoe. Tears slid down his cheeks and dropped off his stubbly chin. Overwhelmed with gratitude, he couldn't speak. Instead, he turned his body toward me and gazed at my face with those same bloodshot eyes. He then opened his food-encrusted, toothless mouth, and smiled. The smell of body odor and alcohol met my nose, but, for some reason, I wasn't repelled by it. My hand no longer reached out to cover my face. Instead, it reached out and touched Johnny's face. And, feeling an unexpected tenderness for him, I smiled back.

"Johnny," I said, feeling the warmth and softness of his skin, "perhaps I have misjudged you too."

That night, in a dark alley in Chelsea, Mass., Johnny Cornflakes helped me learn a profound truth. In God's eyes we are all precious and valuable, every person, every "least of these"—whether we be a shaggy-haired teenager, an unempathetic pastor's wife, or an old town drunk with a new $113.92 shoe.

BACKGROUND SCRIPTURE: Matthew 25:31-40

Denise George is a free-lance writer and author of several books. She lives with her husband and two children in Birmingham, Ala.

7

The Day the Stranger Died

‖ *Death, where is your sting?*
It's naked on a table
in the hospital's stabilization room. ‖

by Dean Nelson

NO SOONER had the barber put the sheet around my neck than the guy in the chair next to me hurled himself to the floor and died.

Sure, we tried CPR, but he had turned a couple of colors before anyone could react. The paramedics hooked him up to the paddles and made it look like they were bringing him back, but when the juice stopped, so did he.

After a few comments to each other like, "What a tragedy," and, "It happened so fast," and, "It's just one of those things," most of us shuffled around the shop in silence. A couple of guys got back in their chairs. I took the sheet from my neck, handed it to the barber, and left.

The scene carried me back to a day when I was a 17-year-old junior in high school, working as an orderly in the emergency room at Hennepin County General Hospital in

Minneapolis. The work was part of a medical biology class, and we were treated by the medical staff as part of the team. We wore scrub suits and even carried stethoscopes so that we could measure patients' blood pressure.

The first night on the job I was hanging around the nurses' desk when I heard an ambulance call in. The paramedic said they were bringing in an unconscious man they suspected was having a heart attack. They estimated they would arrive in five minutes.

I worked with the nurses to set up trays of instruments and machines around a bed in the middle of the stabilization room. No one spoke. Everyone had a task.

Then I went to the parking lot doors and propped them open. I could barely hear the siren as the ambulance sped through downtown. In seconds the siren got very loud, then stopped as the ambulance rushed to the doors. We opened the back of the van and pulled the stretcher out, then rushed down the hall to the room we had prepared.

Someone immediately started cutting the man's clothes off with scissors. Another prepared veins for IVs. Another looked at his eyes with flashlights. And still another stuck needles in his arms. The patient's face was under a thick mask that tried to force air into his lungs. Globs of ointment were slapped on him for the electrocardiogram hookups. Soon the monitors showed us what we already knew was happening.

Nothing.

It didn't take long for the doctors to abandon technology and opt for brute force. One doctor went to pumping the man's chest with such fervor that he was quickly out of breath himself.

"We're losing him," the doctor shouted as he began to use

his fist to try to beat life back into the man. Ten seconds later it was over.

With no pronouncement or discussion, the team quickly began doing their tasks of cleanup. I went to the corner of the room and watched nurses pick up bloody gauze strips and throw away the needles that had started the blood flowing. Technicians unhooked their machines and carefully wrapped the cords around the prongs on the carts so that they would be ready for the next call. Doctors took off masks and gloves and tossed them in the general direction of the trash cans. A nurse handed me a mop to swab up the floor stained with the sickly yellow mixture of blood mingled with ointment and sterilizing solution. Instead, I propped the mop against the wall and backed out of the room into the hallway.

"Doctor, how is he?" the voice behind me asked as I got through the door. I didn't answer because I never dreamed the voice could be talking to me.

"Doctor," the voice said again, this time accompanied by a hand on my shoulder. "How is my husband doing?"

It took me a moment to put this together. I had never seen this woman before. She must have come in a car after the ambulance. All I could do was gape at her. I felt my head begin to nod up and down, yet I didn't want to answer her question. Even then it struck me as offensive that a high school junior would be the first to tell her that her husband was dead. I forced the air through my tightening throat.

"We're doing the best we can," I heard my voice say.

Then I returned to the driveway where the ambulance had stopped. There, I threw up. This wasn't the flu, or botulism, or bad tacos. It was a reaction to what I had just seen.

For 17 years I had acquired a sense of what death must be like. It wasn't just the Ben Casey, Dr. Kildare, or Marcus

Welby shows I had watched, although I'm sure they helped shape some unrealistic views of what dying was like. The people who died on those shows slipped away mercifully for the most part. They often knew it was coming and had made peace with their antagonists.

Nowhere had I seen technicians shear a man's clothes the way a rancher does a sheep. Nowhere had I seen so many needles and machines and bandages and blood and mess. Nowhere had I seen such violence of a doctor in a mask beating on the chest of a patient. Nowhere had I heard such silence. Nowhere had I seen a group change its task so easily and methodically once the goal became unreachable. Nowhere had I felt so sick.

In one 10-minute encounter my body rejected a lifetime of assumptions about what death was like.

I've Found the Sting of Death

Death, where is your sting? It's right there naked in the middle of the stabilization room, like a centerpiece on the table in a horror movie.

Out went the dignity. Out went the last "I love you." Out went the choruses sung at the end of the journey. Out went the notion that we pass from one life to the next. Sometimes we are hurled into it.

Lies, I thought. Everything I was taught about pleasantly crossing Jordan were lies.

I walked to the edge of the parking lot and heard more sirens.

So that's what a siren means, I thought.

And I went back inside.

I don't know of anything—even the birth of my children—that affected me more deeply than this stranger and his widow. For the first time in my life I had to face death, as well as my assumptions about it. The jarring experience didn't scare me away from more contact with death, though. I continued working in emergency rooms in Minneapolis and Kansas City. I even spent a few months on an ambulance crew in Oregon. We helped more people than we hurt; we lost some but saved most. The job never got routine. Yet none of the emergencies I helped with ever reached me the way that first one did.

What amazed me was that at no point did any of these tragedies make me cry. Not when we tried to revive kids who had drowned, or when we tried to keep old people in nursing homes alive until their families got there. It didn't hurt me. It just made me mad.

I guess I thought that God's presence in death would somehow make it peaceful. I'm sure it is peaceful for some—I just never saw it. I guess I thought that having a relationship with Christ meant we could rejoice anyway, for all things were working for good. All I saw was the pain and the heartlessness of it all. From this I concluded that the idea of a big payoff was a cruel hoax. There is no peace as we leave this life, I decided. There is only a surprise ending.

This disturbing view remained with me through college, through the suicides of close friends, and through plane crashes and leukemia that snatched away relatives and colleagues.

Planning to Die

I don't know of any single event that began to turn my attitude back around. I just know that over time I came to realize that we can plan for our mortality. We can't avoid it, so why not accept it? Why pretend my case will be different?

What began to happen was that the cross words I might have spoken at work one day couldn't wait to be resolved in a convenient moment after church or staff meeting or the next day or week or the next time we happened to cross paths. I will not always have the luxury of time and convenience. True, the probability is high that I will have several chances to reconstruct a bridge I just burned, but I can't be sure. It's not worth the risk.

The hurts left from broken relationships became intolerable. I visited some people. I returned things. It wasn't out of a morbid sense of my own impending doom. I just started to understand that death is something I couldn't prepare for in a formal way. So why not do it informally?

I made some mistakes doing this, of course. I called an old girlfriend. I tried to explain why I was calling, but I stumbled around my words a lot and perhaps wasn't as clear as I should have been. We talked a long time, and I'm not sure my wife or my old girlfriend's husband understood what went on in that conversation. I'm not sure I understand it today. All I can say is that there were some unresolved issues that needed resolving. Some doors needed closing. Now they are closed.

A Phone Call Home

As I sat in my office after my nonhaircut, I began envisioning what was happening at the hospital. I wondered if the family knew yet. I wondered if the man's clothes were being cut off or if he was covered with electrodes or if flashlights were being shined in his eyes or if someone was shouting and pounding on his chest.

I wondered if he had a wife who would call an orderly "Doctor" and ask how her husband was doing. I wondered if he and she had argued that morning or if they had parted with a kiss. I wondered if they had said good-night to each other on the last night they spent together, or if they just watched TV or read or sewed or fell asleep in the easy chair and staggered separately to bed in the late hours of the evening. I wondered if they had been obedient to the urging of God to resolve some issues between them and others.

Then I wondered if I had been civil to my wife that morning. Or how we had ended the previous day. I couldn't remember.

I picked up the phone and dialed her office number. At exactly the moment she said, "Hello," I began to cry.

It felt wonderful.

BACKGROUND SCRIPTURE: *Ecclesiastes 7:1-3; I Corinthians 15:50-58; I Timothy 4:13-16*

Dean Nelson teaches journalism at Point Loma Nazarene College, San Diego. He also does free-lance writing for magazines and newspapers, including the *Boston Globe* and *New York Times*.

8

Our Child of Light

|| *"Jeffy will never be able*
to stand, walk, or talk,"
the doctor said. ||

by Jerry Eaton

"YOUR BABY may be in trouble," the doctor said, as Helen was prepped for delivery of our fifth and last child.

Helen had been ill the last weeks of her pregnancy. In desperation, doctors prescribed codeine to stop a hacking cough.

Somehow, I failed to grasp the seriousness of the warning. I was absolutely certain the baby would be a healthy boy, who one day would run for touchdowns and hit home runs just as I had done.

After the birth of our first child, Jerry Jr., there followed three girls—Joann, Jill, and Julie. Helen was 33 years old when she became pregnant with Jeffy. We sensed there would be no more children.

We decided to name our fifth child Jeffrey Kyle Eaton, but we would call him Jeffy. The word *Jeffy* means child of light. To me, the name Kyle suggests masculinity and athletic prowess. I remembered a great football player at Southern Methodist University named Kyle Rote.

So I decided Kyle would be Jeffy's middle name, and Helen agreed.

Jeffy was born shortly after midnight in Manassas, Va., on March 19, 1973. That date was significant because two of his sisters, Jill and Julie, were born on March 18 four years apart.

"Three of our children will celebrate birthdays within one day of one another," I told Helen when I visited her in the delivery room before she was wheeled to her hospital room.

Jeffy *seemed* in perfect health, and I quickly forgot the doctor's warning, "Your baby may be in trouble."

Before long, however, it became apparent that Jeffy, indeed, was in trouble. Our beautiful brown-haired, blue-eyed boy didn't respond to attention, and he didn't progress from one stage of development to another. He didn't roll over or sit up, much less crawl.

Returning to Phoenix, where we lived for years before I pursued a newspaper publishing career in the East, we visited doctors who told us Jeffy was profoundly handicapped. The codeine Helen took affected the blood supply to Jeffy's brain, they said.

"You will need to put Jeffy in a wagon and pull him from here to there because he will never be able to stand, walk, or talk," a doctor told Helen and me.

I've rarely seen Helen weep during our now 27 years of marriage, but she cried after hearing this. However, she wept only once as far as I know. Then she resolved to help Jeffy live his life to the fullest.

Helen's great faith and courage never failed as the weeks

melted into months. My path, though, led to psychological counseling to relieve the hurt I felt.

Jeffy would never score a touchdown or hit a home run. He most likely would never say a word. We would never run together under the sun and fall exhausted in the grass to talk about things important to a father and a son.

A Desperate Prayer

I felt estranged from God, abandoned, and forsaken. Even the bright, cheerful days in Phoenix seemed dull to me. I could hardly endure a cloudy day because it magnified the darkness I felt around me.

I went to bed earlier in the evenings as an escape mechanism, tossed and turned through one unhappy night after another, and awakened feeling drained and sick.

Throughout my life, I have been an overcomer, but I couldn't by the force of my will transform my mentally and physically handicapped son into a normal, healthy person. Moreover, my prayers for Jeffy's healing seemed to fall on deaf ears.

It was then I asked God to take Jeffy if there was to be no healing. One day later, three days before Christmas of 1975—Jeffy was almost three years old—a police officer knocked at our door around 1 A.M. He asked if we had children and if they were accounted for.

Helen and I ran from bedroom to bedroom, gasping as we found Jeffy's room empty. He had crawled out into the near freezing night to play in the yard of the minister across the street. Hearing Jeffy, they summoned police, who bundled him up in blankets. Police drove slowly along the street, looking for a door ajar.

"Here's your Christmas present, lady, three days early," the police officer said, handing Jeffy over to Helen.

After, Helen admonished me. Remembering my request that God take Jeffy, Helen said, "Jerry, you must never again tell God what to do. God returned Jeffy to us always to be our special child."

A few months later, Jeffy actually began to walk. His balance wasn't the best, and his little feet turned inward; but he walked in answer to prayers by his parents, brother, sisters, grandparents, friends, and church members.

Not only did he begin to walk, but he managed to unlock a gate around noon one day and toddle off toward the street. Out of nowhere appeared a dog, fastening her teeth firmly on Jeffy's diaper. The dog held him in place until Helen scooped Jeffy up in her arms.

A tag on the dog's collar identified her as Angel. She left the home of her master, a minister, earlier in the day to appear on our street at precisely the right moment to stop Jeffy from entering a heavily traveled street.

Helen said, "God is using Jeffy as an object lesson to our family about how much He cares for us and protects us."

Jeffy, the Tie That Binds

As months turned into years, Jeffy became the mortar that held our family together. All of us worked with him to help him achieve one tiny victory after another.

Jeffy and I regularly visit Phoenix College to walk around the track, trying to improve his endurance and strength.

I never will forget one hot summer afternoon when a stranger sitting alone in the football bleachers motioned to Jeffy and me.

"You look awfully hot," the pleasant-looking man said. "Here, take a drink of water."

He produced a canteen, and Jeffy and I gulped the cold water. The man—blue of eye and brown of beard—complimented me on having such a wonderful son, waving to us as we continued walking along the track.

"Thanks again," I shouted, turning around to wave at the man, but he was gone. The stands were empty.

Jeffy's sisters manipulate his arms and legs in "patterning" exercises designed to take him through creeping and crawling stages necessary to the development of speech. A normal infant progresses from creeping to crawling and to speech, but Jeffy "skipped" these normal stages of development to simply start walking one day.

It was a mighty day, indeed, when Jeffy at the age of 10 began to say simple words like "Mama." Every time I drive Jeffy to Phoenix College, he repeats the words "Bible book," until I, too, say them.

One evening Jeffy scowled at me as we relaxed in the family room. Running all the words together, he said, "Areyoumadatme?"

"What did he say, Helen?" I asked.

She answered, "He said, 'Are you mad at me?'"

"Jeffy asked a five-word question," I shouted loud enough for the neighbors to hear. It was an event more memorable than an astronaut walking on the moon, as far as I was concerned.

Jeffy normally uses nonverbal communication to compensate for deficiencies in speech. For example, he'll take coins out of Helen's purse around noontime, rummage around for McDonald's hamburger wrappings, and make it clear it's time for a drive to the golden arches to satisfy his endless appetite.

His little room is the happiest in our house. Colored glass objects attached to the ceiling catch the sun's rays, sending patterns of light cascading throughout the room. Jeffy moves from spot to spot in his room to bask in sunlight. He devours picture books, has developed an interest in collecting baseball trading cards, has learned to operate a videotape recorder on his TV set, and swims like an eel in our above-ground swimming pool.

Weekly treatments at a holistic medicine center accelerate his progress.

Applause for Jeffy

God has never once left us without hope for Jeffy's improvement. There have been no flashes of lightning to signify complete and instantaneous healing, but there has always been progress of one kind or another.

We filmed bits and pieces of his life: Jeffy playing with his dogs and cats; the family on picnics at his beloved Phoenix College; Jeffy walking up and down the stairs of the football stadium; Jeffy watching videotaped sports, particularly track; family members hugging Jeffy and singing, "Hooray for Jeffy, hooray for Jeffy. J-E-F-F-Y, J-E-F-F-Y, that's who—that's you!"

"Put your videotapes together for a little movie we want to show at our convention," a doctor at a medicine center in Phoenix told Helen.

The movie was shown on a large screen while excerpts were read from an unpublished manuscript I wrote about Jeffy's life. On the screen the audience saw a little boy—whom doctors once consigned to a wagon—walking, running, and even talking.

There on the screen was Jeffy in his wonderful room, jam-packed with all the things he loves. And there was Jeffy kissing "Mama."

The last scene flickered from view, and the houselights were turned up. The applause started gently and then gathered momentum like a mighty rush of the wind.

Members of the audience began to stand—a few here, a few there, and then the entire auditorium stood and applauded our special child and his supportive family.

Through the years I have learned what it means to praise the Lord, a concept that eluded me for ever so long. God inhabits the praise of His people. The praise frees Him to give us the best from His treasury.

It's not important to me anymore if Jeffy is healed completely. It's enough just to have my boy here, to touch him, to see the smile on his freckled face, and to walk up and down the steps with him at Phoenix College.

BACKGROUND SCRIPTURE: Proverbs 3:5-6; Isaiah 40:27-31

Jerry Eaton teaches at Maricopa Community College in Phoenix and is working on a master's degree at Arizona State University. This chapter is from *Home Life*, December 1988. Copyright © 1988 The Sunday School Board of the Southern Baptist Convention. All rights reserved. Used by permission.

9

Twenty-three and Crippled

*Her husband found the sleeping pills
and with trembling voice
asked her to reconsider.*

by Liz Thompson

I LAY HELPLESS on a doctor's examination table in Amarillo, Tex. The May sunshine streamed in from a nearby window.

Dr. Thomas slowly lifted my left leg to a 90-degree angle. With a flick of his wrist, he twisted the whole leg. Pain radiated from my hip to my toes and through my lower back. I wanted to scream.

"I don't like it," he said and ordered an X ray.

I sighed. Would another X ray reveal anything more than the rest?

After the X ray, I hobbled to the examination room to wait. In what seemed a matter of seconds, Dr. Thomas returned. "Just what I was afraid of," he announced. My heart pounded. With a solemn expression, he walked to the window and held the X ray to the light. Clouds had covered the sun, distant thunder rumbled, and rain began to fall.

Nine months before, I had been exercising in the apartment I shared with my husband, Steve, on the campus of Colorado Christian University, nestled in the foothills just west of Denver. The next morning I awoke with a sore left hip. I assumed I had strained a muscle during the workout, but the pain continued. By October, my hip joint froze for two- or three-day periods. The pain and inflammation inhibited walking and studying, two activities vital to a college student—especially a senior.

From October to February, periods of pain alternated with periods of relief. Some days I enjoyed jogging and skiing as if I were in perfect health. But some mornings, a stiff, throbbing hip dared me to get out of bed.

On those mornings, getting dressed required more energy than a three-mile run. I moved like an instant replay in slow motion. Once ready for class, I would step into the brisk mountain air and limp frantically across campus to my classroom. Arriving late, I would gather my composure in the hall, open the door, and attempt to walk normally to my desk.

Days like that filled the last two months of school. The periods of pain and stiffness lengthened. The doctors I consulted diagnosed a pinched nerve or chronic muscle spasms. I wasn't satisfied with those answers, but I wanted to believe them. By the time spring break rolled around, though, I knew my ailment was serious. Pinched nerves and muscle spasms don't last for seven months, do they?

Denial seemed the only way out. So I pretended to feel good. It's just the stress of upcoming finals, term papers, and graduation that's making my condition worse, I reasoned. Once I'm through with all of those things, I'll be fine.

So I kept jogging, skiing, and adhering to the rigorous schedule of a college student, which included little sleep and skipped meals. I was a productive person, and I refused to let pain stop me.

Muscle relaxers and God's grace carried me through graduation. After that, the pain reached its highest threshold. I lost almost all mobility in my left leg. Weak and underweight, I determined to discover the culprit behind my agony. Leaving Steve behind in an apartment cluttered with boxes to be packed and moved, I flew to my hometown of Amarillo for a consultation with a specialist.

Sitting in the orthopedic clinic, I listened numbly as Dr. Thomas pronounced the diagnosis: a rare form of crippling arthritis. I stared at the X ray in disbelief.

The cartilage that once served as a cushion between the ball and socket in my hip had deteriorated to a thin film. With a Texas drawl, Dr. Thomas said, "Now, honey, you're jist gonna hafta start livin' with your hip instead of makin' it live with you. This is serious."

No, I silently replied. This is a mistake. I'm active. I'm only 23. Only little old ladies in their 60s get arthritis.

But the diagnosis was undeniable. The prognosis: Canes and crutches? Radical surgery? A wheelchair by 30?

As I left the clinic with tears streaming down my face, questions flooded my mind.

What about the 10-K race I planned to run in October? What about those new skis Steve gave me for Christmas? Will they stand in a closet and collect dust? How will this affect my marriage? Will I be able to have children? What about my future ministry? How can I have one if I can't even get out of bed in the morning? How can I, an active person, live a sedentary life?

Life with a Cane

Steve joined me in Amarillo, and we lived with my parents until we found a place of our own. I managed to get around with the use of a cane, but I spent a lot of time in bed, staring at the ceiling, reminiscing about the good old days: the ballet company, the gymnastics team, the track team, the ski trips. All gone! All were stripped from me, by whom or because of what I didn't know.

I kept preaching to myself: Now, Liz, you're a Bible college graduate; you're supposed to be spiritual. You know you shouldn't question God. You're to praise and thank Him for your situation, no matter what it is, and ask Him to use it for His glory.

Psalms, hymns, and spiritual songs? No, thanks. The familiar chorus, "God is so good. God is so good. God is so good; He's so good to me," rattled around inside my head. How could I believe that? I believed my life was ruined. I had no future, and my good God stood by and watched.

In the midst of this period of depression and introspection, I discovered Psalm 73.

The Psalmist Asaph suffered from an infirmity, probably a physical one. Because of his struggle, he wrestled with God's goodness. At the beginning of his lament, he cried, "Surely God is good to Israel, to those who are pure in heart."

Although God blessed Israel when it obeyed, and punished the nation when it disobeyed, Asaph suffered personally, even though he was obedient.

I reasoned like Asaph, If I'm nice to God, shouldn't He be nice to me? I didn't expect a BMW to drop out of the sky and land in my driveway, but I thought God owed me at least health and happiness as long as I played by the rules.

My illness left me disillusioned. What had I done wrong? I probed my memory, hoping to pinpoint the sin that caused my suffering. I thought of none serious enough to qualify.

After many futile attempts to discover the cause of my illness, I faced a decision: Trust God anyway? Or become a cynic? My response wasn't immediate. I had a "Don't call me, God, I'll call You" attitude. Like Asaph, "My feet had almost slipped; I had nearly lost my foothold" (v. 2).

Plans for Suicide

One evening, I was driving home from my parents' house. Intense pain bounced from my hip to my toes every time I moved. "When is this thing going to end?" I sighed.

As I passed a supermarket, the urge to end my life overwhelmed me. I pulled in the parking lot and stopped the car. I can't stand this pain any longer, I thought. Why live with it? I'm tired of this stupid cane; I look like an old lady.

I dread going places. When I walk into a restaurant or a mall, everyone stares. I'm embarrassed when I run into old high school friends. How many times have I lied and said I should be fine in a few months?

I grabbed my cane and limped inside the store. I snuck to the medicine counter, grabbed a box of Sominex, paid, and hurried out the door. I drove home, stunned that I had bought sleeping pills.

The apartment was empty when I arrived, so I tossed the sack on the kitchen cabinet and headed for the shower.

In the meantime, Steve came home. Ready for bed, I walked into the living room and found him holding the box of Sominex.

With trembling voice, he begged me to reconsider. As we

sat on the floor by the fireplace and talked, my feelings poured out. I told him that my illness kept me from fulfilling my role as a wife. I felt guilty because he did most of the shopping and cleaning.

He reassured me that his love for me continued to grow despite the hardship we faced, that he still needed me. He finally got through to me. I realized suicide wasn't the answer. I loved Steve more than I hated the pain.

I continued to wrestle, however, with God's goodness. Asaph wrestled too. In his confusion, he compared his situation to the prosperous, carefree lives of the wicked, and he writhed with envy (vv. 3-12).

I did the same thing as I sat in the locker room at the health club. I watched women my age parade around in their skimpy exercise suits. Their tanned, toned bodies glowed with health. Profanity flowed from their mouths, and they spoke freely of their illicit relationships.

Pale and skinny, I sat on the bench with my cane propped against my leg. "It's not fair," I told God. "Can't You see their pride? They exercise to improve their shapes; I swim to prevent muscular atrophy."

Like Asaph, I concluded, "Surely in vain have I kept my heart pure; in vain have I washed my hands in innocence. All day long I have been plagued; I have been punished every morning" (vv. 13-14). One word described my life: *pain*. The enigma of God's goodness and suffering remained for Asaph as it did for me. The Psalmist could not solve the riddle (vv. 15-16), nor could I.

But something happened when Asaph entered into God's sanctuary. His lament changed to praise when he caught an eternal perspective of his situation. He saw that the wicked will be destroyed swiftly and suddenly, but he would be resurrected into glory (vv. 17–20, 24).

When Asaph stood in God's presence, he realized his ignorance and helplessness. He felt like a stupid animal placed before God (vv. 21–22). Yet God never left his side. Although Asaph questioned God, he placed unconditional trust in Him.

In his book *When Bad Things Happen to God's People,* Warren Wiersbe recalls Elton Trueblood's words, "The fellowship of perplexity is a goodly fellowship, far superior to the fellowship of easy answers." Perplexed like Asaph, I entered God's presence through prayer. In my bewilderment, all I said was, "Help!"

Disease Remains, but God Is Near

Asaph finally understood God's goodness in His presence. He did not have the prosperity of the wicked, but he had the nearness of God (v. 28). He realized that God's goodness was not a thing to be manipulated for his own benefit.

Through Psalm 73, I learned that God's goodness does not depend on my health, but on His character. Hardships such as financial crisis, death, broken relationships, and unemployment do not affect our relationship with Him.

Asaph faced a choice, and so do we. When adverse circumstances arise, will we cash in our faith? Or will we conclude, as Asaph did: "Whom have I in heaven but you? And earth has nothing I desire besides you" (v. 25). God's goodness is His unending presence. "Never will I leave you; never will I forsake you" (Hebrews 13:5).

During the past year, my pain has subsided. Except for a few flare-ups on rainy days, I walk normally and even enjoy some of the activities I once thought impossible.

Yet tomorrow I could wake up crippled again. I have no

guarantee of good health, just as my fellow sufferers have no guarantee of financial success, job stability, or secure relationships. The only thing that's sure is our relationship with God.

Although I still struggle reconciling God's goodness and a believer's suffering, my prayer is with Asaph: "My flesh and my heart may fail, but God is the strength of my heart and my portion forever. . . . It is good to be near God. I have made the Sovereign Lord my refuge; I will tell of all your deeds" (vv. 26, 28).

BACKGROUND SCRIPTURE: Psalm 73

Liz Thompson is studying to become a nutritionist. She lives in Lakewood, Colo., with her husband and two daughters.

10

Ready or Not,
I Was Mom

*She spent time
buying blankets and other accessories.
But the things she needed most
she couldn't buy.*

by Rebecca Laird

FOR THE NINE MONTHS before my daughter's birth, my husband and I prepared for the future. We were getting ready and getting set to launch into parenthood.

About 5:30 P.M. on March 15, I returned from my final prepare-the-nest trip to the shopping center. I was ready. I'd checked off everything on my list, from layette items to a freezer full of easy-to-fix meals. As I began to unpack my shopping bag, I sneezed and felt my first contraction. Was this it?

Contractions and Hall Walking

Eight minutes later I felt the same sensation, a bearable but very real pain. The rhythmic countdown to parenthood had indeed begun. That night before taking off into the unknown, my husband and I calculated our taxes. We wanted to finish all the chores we could, since we didn't know what parenthood would bring.

When I went to bed that evening, I lay there for a while rubbing my very large stomach—soon this part of me would be a baby. What would he or she be like? Would this baby be like a friend or a stranger to me? I drifted off to sleep, and at 2 A.M. my water broke. A few minutes later my husband and I began walking the two blocks up the hill to the hospital.

The doctor checked and verified that I was about to enter motherhood. He then sent me out to join half a dozen other belly-full women trying to find comfortable chairs. Before long we learned the labor rooms were full. The hospital transported us to the medical center across town.

About an hour later I was settled into a gorgeous birthing suite. From this hospital set on a hill my husband watched the dawn break and then the slow approach of barges entering San Francisco Bay from under the Golden Gate Bridge. At least that's what he did between telephoning updates to our family and friends. I, on the other hand, walked the hallways until I could walk no longer. For a day and a half I waited and grew weak. I was ready. Where was that baby?

At 4:22 A.M., 35 hours after that first contraction, an 8-pound, 1-ounce girl with black hair took her first breath and let out a loud, lively squall. Rachel had arrived. Instantly, ready or not, I was a mother.

In Search of a Little Sleep

During the next day friends stopped by to visit. That night, when everyone had finally gone, I determined to keep Rachel in the mobile crib near my bed. I knew the nurses were just the push of a button away. This would be my trial run. But when my child awoke at 1 A.M., then again at 3 A.M., I buzzed the nurse to watch her. Rachel was just 24 hours old, and already I wasn't getting any sleep!

I slept soundly for a couple of hours until the nurse came in early to tell me I could go home at noon. What? They were going to let me take this little person home already? Didn't they know I'd never done this before?

The nursery supervisor handed my husband and me a set of papers and pointed toward the elevator. I kept half expecting the people we passed on the way to the parking lot to say, "Hey, where do you think you're going with that baby?" I was sure they could tell this was my first time at the helm as a parent.

When we went outside in the brisk spring air, questions overtook me. Was she warm enough? What if she got sick? What if we crashed on the way home?

It took us several tries to position Rachel snugly in the car seat that seemed to swallow her body. Once we were settled in the front and looked back, our tiny passenger blinked her alert, bright eyes. She was ready to go.

A Lesson in Intimacy

Over the next days and months Rachel would become my instructor. I'd read some of the best books on parenting, but my daughter alone could teach me how to be her mother.

The initial days of motherhood were exhilarating, but the nights sometimes were frustrating. Why would my child lie awake crying when she was fed, dry, and warm? What did this little creature want? Some nights I would just have to pull myself out of bed and rock her. Over and over I played soothing lullabies—more for me than for her. I learned to sit quietly and simply be there for Rachel. She seemed to want, most of all, to be close to me.

The realization that I was the most essential person in her life filled me with awe and terror. Without me, at this early stage, she would struggle to survive.

After a few weeks I began to trust Rachel to tell me what she needed and wanted. She was certainly trying. It was up to me to be patient with us both as I learned her language.

A Lesson in Ministry

As Rachel began to smile and recognize me and her surroundings, I marveled at her development. Her every action became a momentous occasion, but life itself was routine and a bit mundane.

I was 29, almost 30 when Rachel was born. For years I had jumped out of bed and rushed off to work at a publishing company. I was used to activity, bustle, and intellectual stimulation.

Now I awoke only to face a day of diapers, laundry, messy feedings, and little conversation. As each housebound day began to follow another, I began to get depressed. Some days I felt isolated and alone. I sometimes daydreamed about the times in the past when I was involved in ministry. During this home-centered period of my life, I battled the temptation of longing for more outward activity to validate my life and faith. Why was it so hard for me to settle into this season of motherhood? In my head I knew it wouldn't last long; I wanted to fully cherish these fleeting days, but my mind wandered.

In an attempt to keep my mind active and my spirit alive, I signed up for a nine-month spirituality course that met once a month. During one of the sessions, the leader projected onto the wall a slide of a woman and a small child. The picture had the quality of a portrait of the Madonna hovering over her Child. The image moved me deeply. The intimacy, the focus, the silent interchange between the two sparked in me a new understanding of what ministry meant. The Madonna figure was surrounding the small one with love and presence.

This mother was listening to the unspoken needs of the little one attentively, with her whole heart. Aha, my spirit said. This is what this season of my life is about. As Rachel's mother, I must stay put to surround her with love and presence. For as I minister to her in this way, I allow her to put her energy into the important work of sleep, play, and being alive.

Perhaps being attentive was the most important task of motherhood I could learn. Simply being with my daughter, surrounding her with care, and giving her time, is essential for us both to grow.

A Lesson in Unconditional Love

When Rachel was about 10 months old, I received a letter from a friend. My friend had been struggling with an extended illness. This illness left her with a sense that she was not as important to God as she once had been. She felt ready to serve but unable. Unless she could do something for God, she felt worthless. I understood all too well that trap of thinking one had to achieve, produce, and behave to be loved. As I prayed for guidance on how to respond to my friend, God reminded me of a scene from the breakfast table.

Just that morning, Rachel had woken with a runny nose. Her eyes were bleary and she was cranky. When I made silly noises trying to encourage her to eat a little breakfast, she tried with all her might to smile at me. That smile offered through her suffering meant the world to me. I love Rachel when she is sick, when she is cranky, when she is fun to be around, and when she is not. That morning I saw how unconditionally she loved me too. Even in her suffering she wanted to smile at Mommy.

I told the story of Rachel's smile to my friend. Rachel reminded me how God loves us all. God loves us through runny noses and cranky attitudes. God, like a loving parent, knows us and loves us even when we have little to offer in return. Our desire to smile at God through our troubles is received with pleasure by the One who loves us completely.

A Lesson in Faith

One Sunday evening, a couple of weeks before Rachel turned one, I sat in the living room recalling how lovely the day had been. The morning church service had been wonderful. We'd had lunch with friends who have a daughter near Rachel's age. The two girls had played so well together. Rachel fell asleep for a late nap, so my husband went alone to a dinner hosted by some friends. The spring afternoon was turning cold, so I turned on the heat in our old Victorian house. Hot air billowed up from the floor vents.

Rachel woke up, and we played patty cake and sang her favorite song, "Clap Your Hands, All Ye People." I loved to watch her little hands clap and her face light up with pride as she made off-tune but exuberant attempts at singing. Soon Rachel crawled off my lap and started down the hall. It was dinnertime, so I stood to follow a few steps behind, thinking about what I would feed her.

Rachel was just beyond my sight when I heard her scream. Instantly, I remembered the heat vents in the floor. "Rachel, no!" I cried out, knowing she must have put her hands on the hot metal. But I was too late. Her hands were already seared. I grabbed her and heard my own wailing, "I'm sorry, I'm sorry, Mommy forgot, I'm sorry!" I ran cold water over her red, crisscrossed hands as she screamed and looked at me as if to say, "Make me better, Mommy, it hurts!"

Rachel's coat hung on the doorknob next to my purse. I grabbed them both and ran out the door and up the hill to the hospital. Rachel wailed all the way. The nurses put me in a waiting room, where I paced while waiting for the pediatrician.

Why hadn't I remembered the furnace? As a rule I turned it on only when Rachel slept. I knew it was a hazard. Why hadn't I remembered? What was wrong with me? I felt like a horrible mother.

The doctor came in and assured me Rachel would survive. I would need to apply burn ointment and change her dressings daily, but she would heal—children were resilient. That I could believe, but was *I* resilient?

The doctor advised me to let my guilt motivate me to get down on my knees and crawl around the house, looking for other hazards and rechecking my efforts at child-proofing. Then I should let the guilt go and love my daughter. Despite my best efforts, I would probably be back to the emergency room sometime. Even the best parents can't be omnipresent. Accidents and mistakes happen.

In a couple of weeks Rachel's hands healed, as did my confidence. Even with bandaged hands she crawled over to me and lifted her arms to be held. She didn't blame me. She still loved me.

That emergency taught me how important my faith is as I do my best to be a good mother. I can plan, organize, ask for help, yet still there will be unexpected pain and needs. As

Rachel's mother the most I can do is love her fully, do my best in raising her, and beseech God to surround her with His love and presence.

When I prepared for motherhood, I spent a lot of time acquiring the blankets, crib, and other accessories I would need to care for my child. Yet in retrospect the things I've needed most are things you can't buy: patience to wait for growth, acceptance of God's unconditional love, and faith that He will never leave me or my child.

BACKGROUND SCRIPTURE: *Deuteronomy 31:8; Psalm 139:1-16; Ephesians 2:4-5*

Rebecca Laird is a free-lance writer and editor living in San Francisco.

11

The Day My Son Left the Nest

*I couldn't hide the tears
as we hugged good-bye at Gate 18.
Then Shirley and I drove alone to our house.*

by James Dobson

YEARS have come and gone since the morning of October 6, 1965, when our first child came into the world. An irrational love affair was born that day between this dad and his new daughter, Danae Ann, who took center stage in the Dobson household.

How deeply I loved that little girl. She would stand in the doorway and cry as I left for work, and then run giggling to meet me at the end of the day. Could I ever love another child as much as this one?

Then a little lad named James Ryan made his grand entrance five years later. He was my boy—the only son I would ever have. What joy I felt as I watched him grow. I felt proud to be his father—to be trusted with the well-being of his soul.

I put him to bed every night when he was small, and we

laughed, played, and talked about Jesus. I would hide his sister's stuffed animals around the house, and then we would turn out the lights and hunt them with flashlights and a toy rifle. He never tired of that simple game. But those days have passed.

This morning marked the beginning of the empty nest for Shirley and me. Danae graduated from college a year ago. It was difficult for us to let her go, back in 1983, but we took comfort in Ryan's six remaining years at home. How quickly those months have flown. Today we took Ryan to the airport and sent him off to Colorado for a five-week summer program. Then in August, he plans to enter his freshman year at a college in the Midwest. Though he will be home periodically, our relationship will not be the same. It might be even better, but it will certainly be different. I have never liked irreversible change.

Though for many years I knew this moment was coming, I admit freely that Ryan's departure hit me hard. For the past two weeks, we have worked our way through a massive accumulation of junk in his room. Ryan collects things no one else would want—old street signs, broken models, and favorite fishing rods.

We all took tetanus shots and plunged into the debris. Finally last night, Shirley and Ryan filled the remaining boxes and emptied the last drawer. His suitcases were packed. Our son was ready to go.

Ryan came into my study about midnight, and we sat down for one of our late-night chats. I won't tell you what we said in that final conversation. It is too personal. I can only say that the morning came too quickly, and we drove as a family to the airport.

There I was, driving down the freeway, when an unexpected wave of grief swept over me. I thought I couldn't stand to see him go. I looked forward to what the future held, but I mourned the end of a precious time when our children were young and their voices rang in the halls of our house.

I couldn't hide the tears as we hugged good-bye at Gate 18. Then Shirley and I drove alone to our house, where our son and daughter had grown from babies to young adults.

Home, the Monastery

The house that we had left three hours earlier in a whirl-wind of activity had been transformed. It had become a monastery.

I meandered to Ryan's room and sat on the floor by his bed. His crib had once stood on that spot. Though many years had passed, I could almost see him as a toddler—running and jumping to my open arms. What a happy time that was.

The ghost of a kindergartner was there, too, with his brand-new cowboy clothes and his Snoopy lunch pail. Then a seven-year-old boy appeared. He was smiling, and I noticed that his front teeth were missing. His room was filled with bugs and toads and a tarantula named Pebber.

Then a gangly teenager strolled through the door and threw his books on his desk. He looked at me as if to say, "Come on, Dad. Pull yourself together!"

I remember saying in my second film series, *Turn Your Heart Toward Home,* that the day was coming soon when "the bicycle tires would be flat, the skateboard would be warped and standing in the garage, the swing set would be still, and the beds would be empty. We will go through Christmas with no stockings hanging by the fireplace, and the halls will be very quiet. I know those times will soon be here, and I realize it has to be so. I accept it.

"I wouldn't for anything try to hold back our son or daughter when it comes time to go. But that will also be a very sad day because the precious experience of parenting will have ended for me." Alas, the day that I anticipated has arrived.

If you're thinking I am hopelessly sentimental about my kids, you're right. My greatest thrill has been the privilege of raising them. Still, I did not expect such intense pain at the time of Ryan's departure.

Life, Full of Hellos and Good-byes

When Ryan boarded that plane in Los Angeles, I realized again the temporary nature of life. As I sat on the floor of his room, I heard not only Ryan's voice but also the voices of my mother and father, who laughed and loved in that place. Now they are gone. One day Shirley and I will join them.

Life boils down to a series of happy hellos and good-byes. Nothing is permanent, not even loving relationships. In time, we must release our grip on everything we hold dear. King David said it best, "As for man, his days are as grass: as a flower of the field, so he flourisheth. For the wind passeth over it, and it is gone; and the place thereof shall know it no more" (Psalm 103:15-16, KJV).

If we really grasped the brevity of life, we would surely be motivated to invest in eternal values. Would a 50-year-old man pursue an adulterous affair if he knew how quickly he would stand before God? Would a woman make herself sick from in-law conflict or other petty frustrations if she knew how little time was left?

Would men and women devote their lives to the pursuit of wealth if they realized how soon their possessions would be torn from their trembling hands? When eternal values come in view, our greatest desire is to please the Lord.

If we really believed that the eternal souls of our children hung in the balance today—that only by winning them for Christ could we spend eternity together in heaven—would we change the way we live?

I urge mothers and fathers of young children to keep this eternal perspective as you race through the days of your lives. Don't permit yourselves to become discouraged with the responsibility of parenting. Stay the course.

Get on your knees before the Lord and ask for His strength and wisdom. Finish the job to which He has called you. There is no more important task in living, and you will understand that assignment more clearly when you stand where Shirley and I are today.

In the blink of an eye, you will be hugging your children good-bye and returning to an empty house. That is the way the system works.

BACKGROUND SCRIPTURE: *Psalm 103:15-16; Matthew 6:19-21*

James Dobson is founder and president of Focus on the Family. Adapted with permission from *Dr. Dobson: Turning Hearts Toward Home,* by Rolf Zettersten, copyright © 1989 Word Books, Dallas.

12

The Practical Thing to Do

║ *"Take the bull by the horns* ║
and put us in the nursing home."

by Madge Harrah

A COLD NIGHT WIND buffeted the bedroom windows, hurling sleet against the glass. My father looked up from his pillow and rasped in a hoarse voice, "Madge, I finally have to admit it—your mother and I just can't live here in our own home any longer. You're going to have to take the bull by the horns and put us in the nursing home."

My parents' doctor had said much the same thing to me earlier that day, but my heart still thudded with shock at my father's words. The one thing my aged parents had both been praying for during the past several months was to be allowed to live their remaining days together at home, surrounded by their own things. I glanced toward my mother, who lay next to my father, sharing his bed as she had throughout a lifetime of marriage. Once tall and plump, she was now thin and shrunken from osteoporosis, a disease that makes bones fragile.

A few days earlier I had flown here to my parents' home in southern Missouri from my home in Albuquerque, N.Mex., to help with their nursing care. My father had come down with pneumonia and incipient congestive heart failure, and my mother had developed influenza. Although they managed to pull through that crisis, their doctor had warned me that they probably would not live much longer.

How About the Nursing Home?

"How do you feel about the nursing home, Mom?" I now asked.

I watched her fingers creep across the sheets to clasp my father's large, work-worn hand.

"I'll do whatever you and your father decide," she said.

This is it, I told myself, still not believing it could be true. The time has finally come.

I had been hoping along with them that such a decision would never have to be made. I glanced around the bedroom, which was filled with some of their favorite things: their comfortable queen-size bed with their special individual pillows; the patterned comforter they both liked; my father's brown walnut desk; his old manual Remington typewriter; the large blue vase he had bought as a gift for my mother; and on the walls, some of Mother's best paintings, her gifts to my father. How could my parents be peaceful and happy in any room but this?

"I put our names on the waiting list for the nursing home three years ago," Dad said, his voice taking on some of the authority and strength he had used in the classroom throughout 40 years of teaching. "It's time to put us away."

I had visited that nursing home, which was run by some of my parents' former students. The home was clean, the staff well-trained, the food nourishing, the atmosphere cheerful. If I put my parents there, I knew they would get good care.

I have always believed that people should not feel guilty about placing a loved one in a nursing home. Sometimes a nursing home is the best answer. But in this instance I resisted the idea. For one thing, I was my parents' only surviving child, and I lived over 700 miles away. If they went into that nursing home, they would have no relatives nearby to visit and check on them.

"But I want—," I began.

Dad lifted a hand to stop me. "Look, I know you keep saying we can come and live with you, but it isn't practical. We've got to be practical."

Practical—one of his favorite words.

"Albuquerque is a long way off," he went on. "We're too sick to travel. You've got your own family at home to take care of. No, the practical thing is to put us in that nursing home and not look back."

Dad was right; that *was* the practical thing to do. Then why did I feel so terrible about it? And why did he look so forlorn?

Barely audible above the clamor of the wind and sleet outside, I heard my mother murmur, "I'm going to miss this bed."

Unable to bear their pain any longer, and knowing they both liked a cup of something hot at bedtime, I said, "I'll go make a pot of decaf coffee."

Turning, I fled from the room. After plugging in the coffeepot, I wandered down the hallway and into the living room, where I nervously picked things up and set them down again. My head pounded, my hands trembled. Never had I felt so helpless or so alone.

"All right, God, I need some help here," I begged in silent despair. "Are You listening?"

The only answer was the howling of the storm shaking the house, shaking me. I touched a drawer handle that my practical father had screwed to the wall at hand level. At regular intervals throughout the house were other drawer handles screwed to the walls, put there by my father when he first started losing his balance due to inner-ear trouble. The handles helped him walk from one room to another; he could pull himself from handhold to handhold without fear of falling down. Yes, he was practical, all right. Practical and logical, as a math teacher should be.

OK, then. Let's be practical, whispered a cold, hard voice in the back of my head. If they go into the nursing home, you're off the hook. No bedpans to empty, no lost sleep, no watching them fade away. They're too weak to fly. If you take them to New Mexico, you have to hire a van with a bed for them to lie down on, and you'll have to bring oxygen along. They might die on the trip . . .

But Dad didn't really want to go into that nursing home. Mother had told me so in private, but I would have known it anyway, just from the lost look in his eyes when he talked about it.

On the other hand, moving them to New Mexico would be messy and difficult, and certainly impractical.

"God, You've got to help me!" I cried aloud. "I can't stand this! What's the best thing to do?"

Still no answer.

I wandered on into the dining room where some of Mother's drawings lay scattered on the table, simple line drawings on cardboard. She had made them for the children's Sunday School classes at her church to illustrate various Bible verses. I glanced idly over them and then stopped, arrested by one drawing in particular. It showed a soaring mansion that reached into the clouds. The verse lettered below read, "In my Father's house are many rooms; if it were not so, would I have told you that I go to prepare a place for you? And when I go and prepare a place for you, I will come again and will take you to myself, that where I am you may be also" (John 14:2-3, RSV).

The Impractical Solution?

It was as though light flowed into me, bringing with it a stilling of the storm, a sense of peace. There it was—the answer I'd been praying for.

I scribbled a note to myself and hurried back into my parents' bedroom.

"Now listen," I said to them both, "I will have to put you into that nursing home for the time being, until you get some of your strength back. But meanwhile, I'll hire a mover to take all this"—and I swept my hand through the air to include everything in the room— "to New Mexico. I'll fix up a room in our house, with all your things in it, and when the room is ready and the weather warms up, I'll be back in Missouri to get you."

Although they tried to smile, I saw the doubt on their faces. Would I come back for them? They weren't certain.

Nevertheless, a few weeks later my husband, Larry, and I flew back to Missouri, hired a van, and drove my mother and father to our home in New Mexico. The night after we arrived, I carried a tray with a pot of coffee and two cups into their bedroom, where they lay side by side in their own bed, their special pillows under their heads and their patterned comforter over their frail bodies. Against one wall sat my father's desk and typewriter, along with the big blue vase, and hanging above the desk was mother's painting of a pot of Missouri wildflowers.

"Totally impractical," my father said gruffly when I appeared in the doorway.

Six weeks later my father went to live in the room Jesus had prepared, and four months after that my mother followed.

Recently, in going through boxes that Larry and I brought back after clearing out my parents' home, I came across the note I had scribbled to myself that stormy night back in Missouri after getting the answer to my prayer. The note reads: "Sometimes the wise, sensible, practical solution to a problem is not the best because it leaves out love. Sometimes the illogical, difficult, expensive, messy solution is the best because it's the only way love can be satisfied."

I had chosen the loving solution, and somehow I think my father may have agreed—it was the practical solution after all.

BACKGROUND SCRIPTURE: *John 14:2-3; Romans 13:7-8*

Madge Harrah is a full-time author and playwright. She lives in Albuquerque, N.Mex. This chapter is reprinted with permission from *Guideposts* magazine. Copyright © 1990 by Guideposts Associates, Inc., Carmel, NY 10512.

13

When My Husband Died

Fleeing to her room after a spanking,
eight-year-old Holly fell asleep
with her arms around her dad's picture.

by Sandra Picklesimer Aldrich

IN DECEMBER of 1982, after a hard fight, my husband, Don, lost his 16-month battle with brain cancer. As the Scottish piper played "Amazing Grace," the funeral director closed the casket. I felt as though my life closed in that moment too.

Our children, 8-year-old Holly and 10-year-old Jay, leaned against me as I fought back the tears. I knew if I started crying, I'd never get through the rest of the service.

Fears swarmed around me. How could I go on without Don's loving authority? How could I take over the many decisions that had been his? How could I raise two children alone? What was I going to do? I felt paralyzed.

Married at 20, I had gone from my father's authority to that of my husband. I had never balanced the checkbook, read the tax papers I signed, or made major financial decisions.

From previous grieving relatives I'd already learned anger can keep us from God, deepening our misery. Even though I was devastated by Don's death, and angry at the turn my life had taken, I refused to turn away from my Heavenly Father. Instead I clung to Him all the tighter, drawing strength to face each new day.

In the weeks following the funeral, Philippians 4:19 hovered over me: "And my God will meet all your needs." As the weeks unrolled and I struggled with the unfamiliar territory of decision making, I often challenged the Lord, "Even *this* need?" Gradually I learned to listen to His direction and trust my own common sense.

What helped most was reading the Word. Each evening after I tucked Jay and Holly into bed, I wrapped one of my grandmother's Kentucky quilts around my shoulders and opened my Bible. I was especially comforted by Isaiah 54:5—"For your Maker is your husband." As I struggled with each new responsibility—whether replacing the vacuum cleaner belt or changing the oil in my car—I'd mutter, "OK, You're my Husband now, and I need help figuring this out." As I asked, the Lord's help came.

I also latched onto Jeremiah 29:11—"'For I know the plans I have for you,' declares the Lord, 'plans to prosper you and not to harm you, plans to give you hope and a future.'"

The biblical accounts of women facing tough decisions—especially Esther and Deborah—offered great encouragement. I also looked to those in my life who had faced tragedy. Grandma Katie Lovely had been widowed by a Kentucky coal-mine accident just weeks after her 23rd birthday. She was left with two toddlers and a four-week-old baby, but she had survived and raised her family. So would I. Also, I could be thankful my children were older and had many memories of their dad.

An Ethiopian friend provided another example of strength. When the Marxist government took over her beloved homeland, she and her family escaped just hours before soldiers came to arrest them. In one evening, she lost relatives, friends, position, home, security—even her country. Following her lead, I learned to concentrate on what remained instead of what was lost.

Learning to Laugh

I began coping with decision making and the acceptance of a scary future, but I was convinced I'd never laugh again. Then one evening I read John 16:20, 22. "You will weep and mourn while the world rejoices. You will grieve, but your grief will turn to joy. . . . and no one will take away your joy."

I thought about that for several days. Don had always loved a good joke, so our social gatherings rang with his booming laughter. After he died, I closed myself to humor. But as I moved through grief, I began to appreciate each moment's preciousness and how Don's laughter had drawn people to him—including our own Jay and Holly. Then, at a family dinner, my brother, Mitch, told a story about one of our offbeat relatives. In that moment, I consciously decided to allow laughter to return to my life, and in the process, to rejoin life.

But I had a few bumpy times before I could laugh about the challenges I faced as a suddenly-single parent.

Both Don and I had taught Sunday School, so our Saturdays fell into a routine: I started the laundry while he prepared breakfast. His specialty was French toast. He'd add cream to the egg mixture, dip thick bread into the dish, and cook the pieces on a hot skillet, producing perfect fluffy, golden slices.

After his death, I tried to avoid Saturday breakfast and its memories, making sure we three were either at a restaurant or with relatives. But the day came when I had to face the skillet at last. We were snowed in, so I pulled out the cold cereal. Jay shook his head. "We want French toast." I hesitated, then turned to the breadbox, trying not to think of those Saturday mornings when another cook stood in that spot.

I beat the eggs just the way I had seen Don do, and added the right amount of cream. But the toast came out overcooked on the outside, soggy inside. Well, maybe it would do for two little kids. They didn't say anything but dutifully poured the syrup over the slices. After the first bite, they simultaneously put down their forks.

"This isn't as good as Daddy's," eight-year-old Holly said matter-of-factly, then burst into tears.

"I know," was all I could say as tears welled up in my eyes.

Jay looked at his sister and then me, and quietly left the room. They never asked for French toast again.

Discipline offered another challenge. I had always been the disciplinarian, but after Don's death I put off that responsibility as long as possible. How could I spank them after all they'd been through?

Then, two months later, Holly was rude to Jay and even refused to complete a simple household task.

Her obnoxious behavior continued through the morning until I finally gave her little bottom a couple of swats. She held back tears as she thrust out her lower lip, gave me one of her crushing looks, and stomped upstairs.

I realize now that she was testing me, wondering if our lives would ever get back to normal, but at the time I felt defeated. I sat in Don's orange chair, feeling very tired and very much a failure. When my tears stopped, I quietly went upstairs to see about Holly. She was asleep on top of her bed, her arms wrapped around her dad's picture.

Even though I had done the right thing, tears of guilt fell on the blanket as I pulled it around her tiny shoulders.

Time to Adjust

I had plenty of questions as I struggled with "if only," and wondered what I could have done differently. I finally concluded our only choice in the midst of tragedy isn't *whether* we'll go through it, but *how*. Life had already taught me to say, "Why *not* me?" so I was spared useless cries of "What did I do to deserve this?" Instead I gave my agony to the Lord and asked Him to bring His good out of my pain. I couldn't foresee He would someday allow me to encourage other hurting families; I was too busy trying to muster the strength to cope with grief's surprises.

One of those came in our dining room. For the first several weeks I couldn't serve dinner at the table and face that fourth—empty—chair. Instead, we ate in the family room while we watched TV reruns.

Then I decided I'd dodged the issue long enough. That evening, we three sat at the table and instinctively put our hands toward each other for the blessing. But the round table was too large, and our hands didn't reach. We needed Don there. I covered my face with my hands and sobbed.

The next evening I faced the dinner hour with the same dread. But we needed structure if we were to remain a family, so I insisted we sit at the table again. That time I sat in Don's chair—so I wouldn't have to look at its emptiness—and we didn't hold hands as we prayed. Gradually we became comfortable again in that setting and learned to make adjustments in other situations so that life could go on.

In the years since that lonely meal, I've learned much about allowing the Lord to bring joy back into empty lives. I've also learned that because I'm God's child, He is concerned about every aspect of my life. I like the three verbs in Luke 11:9—"Ask and it will be given to you; seek and you will find; knock and the door will be opened to you." *Asking, seeking,* and *knocking* are words of our action.

As crippling as grief can be, we can—and must—go on. Much as we long to be rescued from problems, we are still responsible for the results. The Lord has promised to help us, but we have to take that first step. Wonderful experiences *are* ahead for us—if we'll allow the Lord to give them to us.

BACKGROUND SCRIPTURE: Luke 11:5-10; Philippians 4:19

Sandra Picklesimer Aldrich recently took on a new challenge by moving her family from New York to become senior editor of *Focus on the Family* magazine in Colorado Springs. She's also the author of *Living Through the Loss of Someone You Love* (Regal, 1990).

Other Dialog Series Books

Building Self-esteem
The Christian and Money Management
Christian Personality Under Construction
Christians at Work in a Hurting World
Christians in a Crooked World
Clean Living in a Dirty World
Coping with Traumas of Family Life
Growing Season: Maturing of a Christian
How to Improve Your Prayer Life
How to Live the Holy Life
Life Issues That Can't Be Ignored
Misguiding Lights? (The Gospel According to . . .)
No Easy Answers: Christians Debate Today's Issues
Questions You Shouldn't Ask About Christianity
Questions You Shouldn't Ask About the Church
Timeless Truths for Timely Living
Tough Questions—Christian Answers
What Jesus Said About . . .
When Life Gets Rough

For a description of all available Dialog Series books, including some that may not be listed here, contact your local bookstore or your publishing house and ask for the free Dialog Series brochure.